"Dillon Burroughs [...] [...]se longing for deep sa[...]

—**Daniel Darling,** author of *iFaith: Connecting with God in the 21st Century* and *Teen People of the Bible: Celebrity Profiles of Real Faith and Tragic Failure*

"In a seemingly arid spiritual climate, there's great need for daily devotions of substance. Dillon Burroughs gives that to us."—**Bruce Ladebu,** founder, Forerunner Global Ministries, and Children's Rescue Initiative

"This yearlong devotional book briefly studies the words of Jesus with pertinent relevance to daily living."—**Cecil Murphey,** author or coauthor of more than 100 books, including *90 Minutes in Heaven*

"With grace, Burroughs guides readers into deeper communion with God and greater compassion for others." —**Marla Alupoaicei,** author of *Your Intercultural Marriage: A Guide to a Healthy, Happy Relationship*

"Grab your Bible and Dillon Burroughs's new devotional. Live in each passage of Scripture, mark your favorite phrases and insights, write your thoughts in the margins, and share online at www.ThirstNoMoreBook.com." —**Catherine Martin,** founder, Quiet Time Ministries

New Hope books
by Dillon Burroughs

NOT IN MY TOWN: EXPOSING AND ENDING
HUMAN TRAFFICKING AND MODERN-DAY SLAVERY,
with coauthor Charles Powell (includes DVD)

A ONE-YEAR DEVOTIONAL JOURNEY

THIRST
NO MORE

DILLON
BURROUGHS

*"Whoever drinks the water
I give them will never thirst."*
—Jesus (John 4:13)

NEW HOPE
PUBLISHERS
Birmingham, Alabama

New Hope® Publishers
P. O. Box 12065
Birmingham, AL 35202-2065
www.newhopepublishers.com
New Hope Publishers is a division of WMU®.

Library of Congress Cataloging-in-Publication Data

Burroughs, Dillon.

  Thirst no more : a one-year devotional journey / Dillon Burroughs.
      p. cm.
  ISBN-13: 978-1-59669-312-8 (sc)
  ISBN-10: 1-59669-312-6 (sc)
  1. Bible--Meditations. 2. Devotional calendars. I. Title.
  BS491.5.B87 2011
  242'.2--dc23

                                    2011025669

ISBN-10: 1-59669-312-6
ISBN-13: 978-1-59669-312-8

N114146 • 1111 • 5M1

DEDICATION

I dedicate *Thirst No More* to my father.

His life encouraged my writing though he never lived to see my published works. He believed in me before a single word had been written. Even before I could recite the alphabet, his steady hand held mine through days of joy and pain. When he faced certain pain in his years with cancer, he smiled through tears to encourage us to stay strong in the Lord. Years after his departure, I find his memory deep within me as one who pointed me toward the heavenly Father. Without his influence, I may have never met the One who gives eternal life; now I know my father and I are separated only in this life, to be rejoined in eternity. Until then, I press on, knowing the same encouragement that touched my life may touch others today. There is a sense in which every word I write continues his life until we meet again in eternity.

Thank you, Dad!
Looking forward to seeing you again.

TABLE OF CONTENTS

INTRODUCTION

"I am a little pencil in the hand of a writing God
who is sending a love letter to the world."
—Mother Teresa

Words matter. Jesus called Himself "the Word."
Light was created when God spoke words.
The Bible is called the Word of God. My personal
journey with words began early. At the age of 6,
I read my first book. At 18, my local paper printed
my first article. But it was not until more recently
I discovered the power of words in my relationship
with God and in service of God.

To mark the new millennium in 2000, I made
a personal goal to journal my time with God each
day. Little did I know that five years later I would
have two boxes of notebooks filled with thousands
of prayers, thoughts, and reflections from those
times of refreshing. In fact, I continued to journal
from that day until well into the days my writing
became my vocation. The daily habit stopped only
because my words had transitioned from a conversation between God and me to articles and books
beginning to touch others around the world.

In the midst of writing for others, my pub-
lishing achieved some degree of what this world

would call "success." I spoke across the country on issues of faith; interviews of my publications reached into the hundreds, ranging from local AM radio stations to major headline television news. Some books would be called "best sellers." Others would win awards. More importantly, many lives were being changed, including mine. Friends would contact me from South Africa, Egypt, Canada, Germany, India, New Zealand, and other far-reaching locations to share where they had found my writings or spoken to others using them. Even "secret believers" among people hostile to Christianity began to share how my words were encouraging their walk with Christ. I felt overwhelmed by both the response and the dedication involved to continue helping others.

Over time, God has chosen to open opportunities to return to my first love of writing meditations of my love for Christ. After years of prayer and seeking the appropriate moment, my dear friend and publisher Andrea Mullins has agreed to publish these writings in this book, *Thirst No More*.

The focus in this title is twofold. First, I seek to highlight the words of Jesus presented in the Four Gospels. As He taught, those who drink from the Living Water will thirst no more (John 4:14). Second, I have sought to use this privilege to help those less privileged. One in eight people on our planet lack access to clean drinking water. My friends at Living Water International are working to change this crisis. Through clean water initiatives, lives are being saved every day in the name of Jesus, our Living Water. A portion of this book's proceeds is being donated to their efforts. You can read more about their work and how to help in the back of this book or at www.water.cc.

Before you plunge in, let me also share my desire for this book—changed lives changing lives. To my knowledge, I know of no devotional book that seeks to connect its readers in daily community. *Thirst No More* seeks to be the first. Each day (beginning January 1, 2012), we will experience the privilege to journey together each day at www.ThirstNoMoreBook.com. I encourage you to share your thoughts and to encourage others who share along the way.

For those like myself who prefer to read on screens or on the go, this book is also available as an ebook and can be read from your computer, ereader, or mobile device. Whether you read it on a screen or in print, you can submit your thoughts to the community from any online device, allowing us to share our daily experiences along the journey from wherever God speaks to you.

Finally, please know I pray for you and all of my readers every day. Your intimacy with Christ is my great pleasure. May you truly experience a life in which you thirst no more because our Lord has become your Living Water. May God shine His grace upon you as we share these words together.

"Jesus the Messiah the son of David."
—Matthew 1:1

Genealogies appear mundane. Unimportant. Trivial. But the family line of Jesus is anything but insignificant. The opening words of the first Gospel unearth two critical traits of the coming King.

First, Jesus is called Messiah. Messiah was the term for the Coming One foretold of by the prophets. He would right every injustice. Second, Jesus is called the son of David. Only a man descended from David could fulfill the prophecies of Messiah. Only a king descended from the royal Jewish lineage could rule from the throne of David in Jerusalem.

Jesus came from heaven to earth. King was a step down for Him. Yet He came to fulfill God's Word, to live God's plan, and to show God's love, to me and to you.

Share your experience now at
www.ThirstNoMoreBook.com.

"He will save his people from their sins."
—Matthew 1:21

The name "Jesus" is a variant of Joshua, meaning "God saves." His name included His mission. From before His birth, His purpose had been foretold.

We, too, have been providentially created with a unique purpose. In one sense, we exist to further the purpose of Jesus, to point people to the saving power of Christ. Yet each of us has our own specific vocation, a sacred journey prepared by the Creator of the universe. How can we discover this purpose? The more closely we listen to Jesus, the more clearly we hear His voice. The more closely we sit in His presence, the more clearly we see Him and His plans for us. He longs to share His life with and through our lives today.

Share your experience now at
www.ThirstNoMoreBook.com.

"They will call him Immanuel."
—Matthew 1:23

Immanuel. The Hebrew word means "God with us." The eternal Creator of the universe stepped out of eternity past and into space and time. The designer of human anatomy limited Himself to a human body to one day allow that same body to be beaten and bruised on our behalf.

Ancient words often leave us confused. *Immanuel* should not be among them. Immanuel is the clearest expression of love available, for it communicates Someone greater coming to someone lower for the purpose of love. When God came to us, He revealed His love. When we share in life "with" others, we too reveal His love to them. *God with us* becomes *God in us* and through us as we share this unparalleled love.

Share your experience now at
www.ThirstNoMoreBook.com.

"Where is the one?"
—Matthew 2:2

In some unknown manner, the Magi observed a new king had been born. To honor this Ruler, they sought Him. Their journey would be long, but their destination would be worthy. In their effort, these Magi spoke to many in their travels, asking, "Where is the one who has been born king of the Jews?"

Seeking requires a journey. A search requires a journey. These ancient leaders leave us a pattern to follow yet today. To find the Lord, we must look for Him. To honor Him, we must humble ourselves before Him. When we find our King, we bring Him our gifts. We offer Him our worship. We declare Him as the destination of our journey. He alone is worthy. What is it you bring to the King?

Share your experience now at
www.ThirstNoMoreBook.com.

January 5

"In Bethlehem in Judea."
—Matthew 2:5

The Jewish leaders already knew where the Messiah would be born. Why? Ancient prophecies from the Jewish prophets revealed the location—Bethlehem. In fact, these priests sat only a few miles from where Jesus was born. Yet they missed His coming. Instead, non-Jewish Magi from the East were the ones to seek Him, traveling for weeks to greet His arrival.

Jesus is not a mystery, but He reveals Himself to those who seek Him. Many sit in pews for years and never truly seek Him. Others have never entered a cathedral yet have called out to His Name. Those who seek Him find Him. He is near. We only need to reach out to find Him. He will reveal Himself to us when we do.

Share your experience now at
www.ThirstNoMoreBook.com.

"They bowed down and worshiped him."
—Matthew 2:11

The Magi traveled hundreds of miles in search of one child. They consulted the king and religious teachers in pursuit of this King of the Jews. Further, they did not come empty-handed. Their gifts—gold, frankincense, and myrrh—represented a tremendous commitment.

In comparison, the locals had given the family of Jesus only a manger for a delivery room. The occupying ruler sought to kill the Child. Only shepherds and a few others recognized this baby for who He truly was. When the Magi found the Child at the end of their journey, they did not retell the difficulties of their trip, but rather bowed and worshiped. Only the King mattered. When we experience Christ, all that matters at that instant is Him. Worship Christ.

Share your experience now at
www.ThirstNoMoreBook.com.

"Out of Egypt I called my son."
—Matthew 2:15

Jesus was not only born in an unfamiliar town; He was temporarily raised in foreign territory. In modern terms, Jesus was an immigrant. Many Jews lived in Egypt at this point in history; Jesus and his family were among them. Often belittled by the locals, Jesus was likely mocked and made fun of from His earliest human memories.

This was no mistake; it was a deliberate aspect of God's plan. Jesus endured suffering to fulfill prophecy, suffering that included being the end of racial slurs and immigrant mockery. He knew how it felt to feel small and insignificant despite His position as Lord. When we feel unimportant, we must recall Jesus knows our hurt. He has been there and loves us with perfect, unfailing love.

Share your experience now at
www.ThirstNoMoreBook.com.

"He went and lived in a town called Nazareth."
—Matthew 2:23

Nazareth was a small town. Scholars estimate fewer than 300 people called Nazareth home at the time Jesus lived there. In obscurity, the Son of God learned to read, to build, to work with his hands. The few friends His age would likely have wrestled with the young Jesus without knowing the significance of moment. His parents would pray to God with the Son of God in their presence.

Much of life appears mundane at the time. Yet in God's providence every moment includes significant details arranged by His divine hand. A meal is not only a meal; a conversation is far more than its words. Take time to be aware of God in the quiet moments. Worship Him.

Share your experience now at
www.ThirstNoMoreBook.com.

*"Repent, for the kingdom of heaven
has come near."*
—Matthew 3:2

John began his message with one word—*repent*.
To repent means to turn, to change. Why repent?
"For the kingdom of heaven has come near." The
arrival of Jesus marked the next step in God's plan.
To prepare, John called his hearers to change and
prepare for action.

To follow Jesus today also requires repentance.
We cannot truly follow Him without an unreserved
change of perspective from self to service. Only
when we become servants of Christ have our
hearts adjusted to the proper attitude. Only then
are we prepared for the work of the kingdom of
heaven. Do not stop with faith in Christ. Continue
with change in Christ. Then you will be prepared
for coming kingdom of heaven.

Share your experience now at
www.ThirstNoMoreBook.com.

JANUARY 10

"John's clothes were made of camel's hair."
—Matthew 3:4

John did not fit in with his culture. In fact, his clothing stood out so much that Scripture highlights his fashion choice: "John's clothes were made of camel's hair, and he had a leather belt around his waist." Yet people came to him from the entire region to the Jordan River. Why? To be baptized.

Why did many flock to John for baptism? He offered confession of sins. We may not like to admit it, but we deeply desire to confess our wrongdoings. In speaking our flaws, we relieve ourselves from a burden of secret lusts. Let us confess our sins to our Master today, and to another person if necessary. Let us confess our sins, repent, and seek the Coming One this day.

Share your experience now at
www.ThirstNoMoreBook.com.

"Produce fruit in keeping with repentance."
—Matthew 3:8

John's harshest words were spoken to religious leaders. They knew the promises of God, yet refused to conform to His ways. In response, John commanded them to "produce fruit in keeping with repentance."

This same original word for "fruit" can also be understood as "results." The challenge was to live what they claimed to believe. This message convicts us still. We may believe the right things, but do we live the results of these beliefs? If not, we are in the same situation as the religious experts of John's time. Our transformation must be the same as well—produce fruit. Let us live what we say we believe. Only then are we "keeping with repentance," changing in light of the hope within us.

Share your experience now at
www.ThirstNoMoreBook.com.

JANUARY 12

*"After me comes one who is
more powerful than I."*
—Matthew 3:11

Humility is a mark of genuine faith. John knew his role and clearly communicated that there was one "more powerful than I." John baptized with water; Jesus would share the Holy Spirit. We are servants of our Master's will; Jesus is our source of power. Any time we attempt efforts in our mere humanness, we lack the essential empowerment to accomplish the task.

Scripture is clear that apart from God, we can do nothing. Yet with God, all things are possible. This contrast should humble us, just as it did in John's life, to speak what God wants us to speak; to serve only as He would bid us to serve. In humility, we find our true calling and our greatest honor.

Share your experience now at
www.ThirstNoMoreBook.com.

"Jesus came...to be baptized by John."
—Matthew 3:13

Jesus approached baptism with the same humility He gave to other pursuits. But John knew he did not deserve to baptize Jesus. To baptize the Messiah appeared inappropriate; to Jesus, baptism stood as essential for Him.

Why was Jesus baptized? Much can be said, but one reason was "to fulfill all righteousness." Baptism was part of God's plan; it was right; it was necessary.

Today many view baptism as either the door to Christianity or merely a symbol. The true answer, however, lies mysteriously in between. Baptism is the mark of our repentance, a sign of our allegiance to a kingdom not of this world. Jesus leads this kingdom, a movement calls each of us to embrace and serve. Only through such humility can we please our King.

Share your experience now at
www.ThirstNoMoreBook.com.

"This is my Son, whom I love."
—Matthew 3:17

God is love. He loves us. He also displays love toward Himself between the persons in the Godhead. In a manner without comparison, God the Father declared His love for God the Son in the presence of God the Spirit. All of Trinity revealed itself at the starting point of Christ's public ministry.

Included in this unique allegiance of love is a pattern for us to reflect. If God the Father can openly voice His love for Jesus, should we not do the same? It takes a certain level of effort to communicate love to Jesus in private; it takes a higher effort to speak our love of Christ to a watching world. Speak your love of Christ to others today.

Share your experience now at
www.ThirstNoMoreBook.com.

"With him I am well pleased."
—Matthew 3:17

Jesus pleased His heavenly Father. Of all the words the Father could speak from the sky on the day of Christ's baptism, He ended "with him I am well pleased." There is something deep within the soul that desires to please our earthly father. Whether deserving or not, a father's approval endures as one of the deepest of human longings.

To hear "with him I am well pleased" must have caused Jesus to smile. Such joy, such love. The Father loves us with this love as well. Though His love is unconditional, His pleasure comes when we follow His will in gentle humility. Are you living today in a way that causes our Father to say of you "I am well pleased"?

Share your experience now at
www.ThirstNoMoreBook.com.

"Jesus was led by the Spirit...to be tempted."
—Matthew 4:1

Temptation does not escape God's attention. He knows when we struggle. In fact, at times He sends us into the heat of intense spiritual battle. As with Jesus, temptation stands as a step in our journey in holy pilgrimage.

Our response to temptation reveals the substance of our faith. When we say yes to sin, we remove our eyes from God for momentary human pleasure. When we resist, we say yes to God's pruning, emerging stronger from the process.

God does not desire sin in our lives, yet He sometimes allows temptation as a test. When we pass, He extends trust and we take the next step in our journey. Walk today as one who passes the test; continue your steps in holiness to God.

Share your experience now at
www.ThirstNoMoreBook.com.

"He was hungry."
—Matthew 4:2

Jesus hungered. Though God in human form, Jesus struggled with hunger pangs. His humanity received a challenging test. Forty days of no food opened an opportunity for the temptation to turn rocks into bread.

Of course, Jesus could have created bread from the sky. He was there when manna fell to feed God's people for 40 years in the wilderness. It was not a matter of power, but priority. Jesus was asked to create food for Himself during a time when the Spirit had led Him to live without.

Hunger challenges our lives in a myriad of ways, including choices that bypass God's will for our lives. Live today as one who follows Christ's example and does what God desires, not what our body craves.

Share your experience now at
www.ThirstNoMoreBook.com.

"It is written."
—Matthew 4:4

The best response to temptation is God's Word. How can we know? Jesus, the Son of God resisted the temptations of the devil three times with the phrase "It is written." What is written? God's Word.

Temptation does not require new revelation; it requires attention to God's revelation. When facing a difficult choice, do not ask, "What should I do?" without first asking, "What has God revealed?" This probing question will rescue us from a variety of temptations designed to harm our relationship with God. His truth points out untruth; His ways prepare our ways. In leaning on God's Word, we not only resist but reach deeper in our knowledge of our Father, depending on Him for the strength we desire.

Share your experience now at
www.ThirstNoMoreBook.com.

"Man shall not live on bread alone."
—Matthew 4:4

Bread is used throughout the sacred text as a basic life necessity. Yet Jesus observed bread is not enough for life. Something more is needed.

What is this "more"? To hear from God. To experience Him. Every person longs for a connection with something more than we "see" in this world. This desire can only be adequately fulfilled in God. To hear His voice is greater than any food. To meditate on His words far surpasses the greatest feast.

In this moment, pause to consider the attention we give to God's Word. Is your soul full or is it starving for the "meat of the Word"? Adjust accordingly, for God sees the heart. He knows those who are satisfied in Him. Feast in His Word.

Share your experience now at
www.ThirstNoMoreBook.com.

"Every word that comes from the mouth of God."
—Matthew 4:4

Many of us read from Scripture, but do we treasure every word? Our spiritual hunger is satisfied not only on some words from God, but on every word. From "In the beginning" to the concluding "Amen," every word is a word of nourishment.

As we embark upon the next step of our sacred journey, consider how God's Spirit would guide us to reflect upon "every word." When will we meditate, and where? How will we proceed, at what pace, and on which page? Start today. Begin the next step in your journey and be filled with the food that feeds the soul. Only then can we live fulfilled, wholesome lives in the Spirit. Only then can we resist temptations and rest in God's truth.

Share your experience now at
www.ThirstNoMoreBook.com.

"If you are the Son of God."
—Matthew 4:6

Doubt is among the most sinister of Satan's schemes. Through doubt come discouragement, dismay, and depression. One of his greatest temptations to Jesus was to cast doubt on His identity: "If you are the Son of God."

It has been said when Satan reminds us of our past we should remind him of his future. As children of God, we have eternity with Christ to anticipate. Satan's time is short. His future is dark. When he casts doubt on our identity in Christ, take strength that our future is secure. Our momentary troubles do not compare to our eternal joy. His momentary troubles will end in his eternal destruction. Do not doubt who you are in Christ. You are His child.

Share your experience now at
www.ThirstNoMoreBook.com.

"Do not put the Lord your God to the test."
—Matthew 4:7

The answer to the temptation of popularity is humility. Jesus could have propelled Himself to celebrity status at any time, but He chose the will of His Father. When the devil pressed Jesus to prove His supernatural abilities, He answered, "Do not put the Lord your God to the test."

What test did Jesus have in mind? He specifically resisted the enticement to promote Himself at the expense of God's mission. This application extends to us as well. Through God's Spirit, we have access to power and gifts that could provide status beyond our peers. However, this is not God's desire. His will includes a life of devotion to His glory, promoting Him rather than our own lives. How are you pointing others to God?

Share your experience now at
www.ThirstNoMoreBook.com.

"Away from me, Satan!"
—Matthew 4:10

Jesus holds authority over Satan. This is made clear when Jesus commands Satan to flee and Satan obeys. But why didn't Jesus send the devil away before this third temptation? The answer may lie in the rest of Christ's response: "Worship the Lord your God, and serve him only."

Our Lord endured agony for 40 days in the wilderness for a purpose. In the end, He directed attention to the Father. The Lord who rescued His people from Egypt to their new land also brought Jesus through the wilderness to His new mission. This almighty God used this time to prepare Jesus for the spiritual work in the accounts to follow. When you are tempted today, do not look to human strength. Turn to Christ's triumphant power.

Share your experience now at
www.ThirstNoMoreBook.com.

"Angels came and attended him."
—Matthew 4:11

Temptation is a spiritual battle. The proof? When Satan fled, the temptation of Jesus did not yet end. It concluded with angels. Angels attended or served Him after He resisted Satan's three luring offers.

But why angels? Jesus was God in human form. Did He require the assistance of heavenly beings? In one sense, no. But Scripture shares this truth for our insight, revealing the involvement of God's unseen spiritual forces in our daily battles. God not only knows our struggles; He helps us through them. When we are tempted this day, let us not think God has abandoned us; let us rest assured He and His angels work on behalf of us, His children. God is on our side.

Share your experience now at
www.ThirstNoMoreBook.com

"Jesus began to preach."
—Matthew 4:17

John had been arrested. His followers would have experienced doubt and confusion. What would happen next? Didn't John teach the kingdom of heaven was near? Was his message true? Would the Messiah soon appear?

John's imprisonment turned into the open door for Jesus to preach. The message? The same—"Repent, for the kingdom of heaven has come near." John spoke of the coming Messiah; Jesus spoke as the coming Messiah. John would decrease; Jesus would increase. Likewise, God calls each of us to serve for only a season. We know not when our time will end. Until our time, we must stay on mission, knowing the time is short. Jesus will return. We know not when. We are called to serve until then.

Share your experience now at
www.ThirstNoMoreBook.com.

"I will send you out to fish for people."
—Matthew 4:19

Two brothers, Simon and Andrew, had grown up fishing. Casting nets stood etched in their earliest childhood memories, serving as a daily ritual in their adult work life. When Jesus began to preach in their area, Simon and Andrew would certainly have heard the news. A new rabbi was in town, speaking as John had, announcing the kingdom of heaven was near.

What these two siblings did not know was their new role in God's plan. They had been trained to catch fish. Christ would now call them to fish for people. Would they obey? We are told they left their nets and followed Him. Christ calls us to follow Him as well. Will we lay down our "nets" and follow Him?

Share your experience now at
www.ThirstNoMoreBook.com

"Jesus called them."
—Matthew 4:21

James and John prepared for another day of fishing with their aged father. Preparing their nets, their routine began with folding and cleaning, packing and preparing. Then Jesus came. Jesus changed everything. With one challenge, their careers were transformed into a calling.

Why? "Jesus called them." They left their boat and their father to follow Christ. Nothing else compared with the opportunity to serve the Messiah. Only unrestrained devotion stands as the proper response to the voice of Christ. Christ calls us today. Are we willing to leave our work or even our family—if need be—to respond? Are we prepared to step away from our lives to the life our Lord has designed for us? Jesus requires our utmost allegiance. Choose Christ above all today.

Share your experience now at
www.ThirstNoMoreBook.com.

"News about him spread all over."
—Matthew 4:24

Good news is contagious. Changed lives change lives. As Jesus taught and healed the sick, people talked. With only word of mouth, an expanding range of villagers heard of this new rabbi who could take away disease. Lepers began to hope. Mothers of sick children began to praise God. Perhaps this new teacher could be their answer.

Hurting people seek hope. Jesus offers it. Even in our generation, those who suffer seek solutions to their pain; the ailing desire answers. In Christ, we have the One who can provide what is lacking; in Christ, we know the Great Physician. As we encounter hurting individuals in our lives today, let us remember to speak of our Healer and spread the news about Him all over.

Share your experience now at
www.ThirstNoMoreBook.com.

"He began to teach them."
—Matthew 5:2

When acclaim comes our way, the temptation is to enjoy every moment of it. Sign the autograph; speak to the fans. But as Jesus drew a crowd, He spotted a teachable moment. Rather than looking to His fans for approval, He sat with His closest followers. He taught them.

The applause of the audience is short-lived. When calls resound for an encore, we are called to direct our attention to our Master. These moments reveal whether our true commitment stands for our Savior or ourselves. Jesus knew the best time to share spiritual truth was when His followers were most attentive; let us look for such times among those in our lives, sharing His truth at just the right time this day.

Share your experience now at
www.ThirstNoMoreBook.com.

"Blessed are the poor in spirit."
—Matthew 5:3

Blessed" stands as a traditional term we could also roughly render as "happy." Seen this way, the poor in spirit are joyful. This apparent paradox marks the first of several phrases shared by Jesus to express the marks of true joy. Speaking to the downcast of His day, Jesus began, "Blessed are the poor in spirit."

What does it mean to be poor in spirit? The poor of Jesus' time were those with little income, just as today. "Spirit" indicated an attitude. A person with a weak or lowly feeling was what Jesus expressed. If we are discouraged or feeling down, we can qualify as poor in spirit. We can receive the kingdom of heaven. Why? We are among those willing to respond to the call of Jesus.

Share your experience now at
www.ThirstNoMoreBook.com.

"Blessed are those who mourn."
—Matthew 5:4

Blessed and *mourn* are two words that rarely stand together. Yet Jesus equates the two attitudes. Why? The outcome: "They will be comforted." Mourning is an emotion no one desires. We prefer blessing, or joy. But to those who do mourn, Jesus provides comfort.

Christ is the only One who can give ultimate peace during the loss of a loved one. He is the greatest relief in times of pain or sorrow. Further, Christ's comfort fulfills the predictions of a Messiah who would comfort His people. Only the Chosen One of Israel could answer the needs of God's people. Only the Son of God could identify with the pain of His people. If we mourn, we are blessed. Christ will comfort us.

Share your experience now at
www.ThirstNoMoreBook.com.

February 1

"Blessed are the meek."
—Matthew 5:5

A meek person is a humble person. The one who is humble does not boast, often because the humble person lacks abundance. In contrast, those who live as if they have little will inherit the earth. This contrast marks the way of Christ, who brings down the proud, yet exalts the lowly.

This teaching by Jesus would have much impact on His followers in the days ahead. They would ask to sit at His right and left in the kingdom. He would endure a cross of shame. They would deny Him. Jesus would suffer on their behalf. Jesus did not only teach the blessing of the meek; He lived it. He rules the earth; those who follow Him will share in inheriting the earth.

Share your experience now at
www.ThirstNoMoreBook.com.

*"Blessed are those who hunger
and thirst for righteousness."*
—Matthew 5:6

Hunger and thirst dominate much of our humanity. Without food or water, we cannot last nor thrive. The same is true or our souls. Apart from Christ, our souls starve and slowly atrophy. Blessed are those who hunger and thirst for righteousness.

This righteousness is not about getting even; it is about pleasing God. Rather, His righteousness is of the soul. When our souls hunger and thirst for the Messiah, we will be filled. Nothing less can satisfy. We must refuse to accept satisfaction in our world's substitutes or live as if we can thrive apart from the daily bread of our Savior. He is the Bread of life; He is the Water of life. Only in Him do we find genuine satisfaction.

Share your experience now at
www.ThirstNoMoreBook.com.

"Blessed are the merciful."
—Matthew 5:7

Mercy. The word brings to mind compassion, sympathy, benevolence. But what does it mean to be merciful? Moses taught the Lord is a merciful God for He will not abandon or destroy. God does not treat us as we deserve, but as He desires. He grants mercy because of His great love, a love beyond comprehension or understanding.

For us to be merciful is to treat others not as they deserve but rather as Christ would. The One who taught us to turn the other cheek, the One who demanded we forgive 70 times 7, and the One who died upon a cross for our sins calls us to show similar mercy. Who can we show mercy to this day? How can we show Christ's compassion?

* Some translations say "seventy-seven times."

Share your experience now at
www.ThirstNoMoreBook.com.

"Blessed are the pure in heart."
—Matthew 5:8

What does it mean to be "pure in heart"? A pure heart is a clean heart. No one can enter the presence of God unless his or her sins have been forgiven, with a heart made pure. In earlier times, sacrifices were made and priests were required to enter the presence of the Lord. But then Jesus came. Jesus changed everything.

In Jesus, we can have access to the Father. He has the ability to forgive our sins and provide a way to the Father. How can we be pure in heart? Come to the Son. Receive His forgiveness. Be cleansed. Then we will experience God now and see Him throughout all eternity. We will be truly and eternally blessed. Return to Jesus; be cleansed anew this day.

Share your experience now at
www.ThirstNoMoreBook.com.

"Blessed are the peacemakers."
—Matthew 5:9

Who is a peacemaker? One who makes peace. To make peace is not a passive endeavor, but rather and activist mindset that works toward the end of conflict. In our world, it is not the soldier but the activist who calls for peace. It is the teacher, not the general, who proclaims peace. It is the child of God between warring parties—who makes peace.

The notion of peace is often misused, but at its core peace is a lack of war, an absence of strife. Only a child of God can truly live peaceably. Why? Because only God's children have experienced the true peace that comes from the Holy Spirit. We know there is more to life than desire, than greed. We have encountered a better way, a higher way. We have met the way, Jesus Christ.

Share your experience now at
www.ThirstNoMoreBook.com.

*"Blessed are those who are persecuted
because of righteousness."*
—Matthew 5:10

Persecution thrives in a variety of forms. Torture. Arrest. Death. Ridicule. Discrimination. Regardless of which type, persecution continues among God's people. In fact, Scripture promises anyone who desires to live a godly life in Christ Jesus will be persecuted.

The key phrase here is "because of righteousness." It matters little if we suffer for doing wrong. This is to be expected. But if we suffer for doing what is right, we are blessed. Why? We will receive the kingdom of heaven. This is proof we will commune with Christ for eternity. Persecution is not to be desired, but is to be expected. If you suffer today for your faith, you are blessed. Great is your reward, the eternal reward of the kingdom of heaven.

Share your experience now at
www.ThirstNoMoreBook.com.

"You are the salt of the earth."
—Matthew 5:13

In ancient times, salt was used primarily as a preservative. Salt cured meats, providing flavor that otherwise would not exist. When Jesus called His hearers the salt of the earth, He indicated that they provided flavor to others on His behalf.

On the negative side, if salt loses its flavor, its saltiness, it is no longer good for anything. Jesus taught salt gone bad was salt thrown out. We have the opportunity to live as salt that makes the message of Christ more appealing. We also have the opportunity to live as salt gone bad. Which will we choose? Let us live in a way that highlights the greatness of our Lord and King. Let us flavor His message to a world hungry for spiritual truth.

Share your experience now at
www.ThirstNoMoreBook.com.

"You are the light of the world."
—Matthew 5:14

Unlike in our world, light in ancient times required significant effort. When the sun set, darkness dominated. A single light from a fire or lamp could shine for miles. Several lights burning in one hillside town would glow as a beacon for many to see.

Jesus told His listeners, "You are the light of the world." Just as a light causes a city to stand out or a lamp fills a room with brightness, our lives are to shine God's glory to those in darkness. God floods our lives with light not to keep behind our window, but to share with our world. Jesus lives in us so He can live through us. Shine His light through your life today.

Share your experience now at
www.ThirstNoMoreBook.com.

"That they may see your good deeds."
—Matthew 5:16

We are not saved by good deeds; we are saved for good deeds. Jesus transforms us to transform others. Just as light guides others along the path, our lives must guide those in darkness in the right direction.

Is it wrong to keep the light to ourselves? Would we walk through the forest at night and light the path only for our own steps or would we help others along the way? God expects us to help. How can we help? It begins by living the life of Christ "that they may see your good deeds." Through our actions, God will open up interactions to communicate His wonderful, powerful grace. Through our lives, God will change lives. Through our deeds, God will perform His deeds. We only bear fruit by staying connected to the branch.

Share your experience now at
www.ThirstNoMoreBook.com.

*"I have not come to abolish them
but to fulfill them."*
—Matthew 5:17

Exodus. Isaiah. Zephaniah. Such books can cause even mature followers of Jesus to groan, desiring rather the words of Jesus or His apostles to the weighty thoughts of the Law and Prophets. Yet Jesus did "not come to abolish them but to fulfill them."

In virtually every page of the Jewish Scriptures is an arrow pointing toward the coming Messiah, Jesus. The Coming One becomes the One who came in Matthew, Mark, and beyond. When we read the ancient words, our faith grows stronger as we find the voices of the past presented the fulfillment found in Jesus. Jesus, the One who has come, will come again, giving us great confidence for our lives now and each day. Every word of God is perfect.

Share your experience now at
www.ThirstNoMoreBook.com.

"Not the least stroke of a pen,
will by any means disappear."
—Matthew 5:18

One accusation made against Jesus was that He changed the Law of Moses. This act, considered blasphemous, would be part of the conspiracy that later led to His murder. Yet Jesus clearly taught the enduring importance of God's Law. The least stroke of a pen referred to the smallest dot noting the difference between letters in the Hebrew alphabet. Not even the smallest change would be made to the Law until its fulfillment.

We, likewise, cannot be found to change God's Word. Rather, we must allow God's Word to change us. We must conform to Christ's image, not conform Him to ours. Only then are we obedient to His Word. May we love His Word and live His Word every breath of this day.

Share your experience now at
www.ThirstNoMoreBook.com.

FEBRUARY 12

"Whoever practices and teaches these commands will be called great."
—Matthew 5:19

Jesus modeled simplicity. He owned no house. He walked from one location to the next. He ate common foods. When Jesus taught, people also listened. In the same simplicity, Jesus made clear the requirement "whoever practices and teaches."

In our modern world, we often separate faith from practice. But the way of Jesus rejects this notion. Only living our faith offers the credibility to teach our faith. Anything less is less than the teachings of Christ. Those who combine faith and action are called great in the kingdom of heaven, the only reward worth pursuing in this life. Live to be called great in God's kingdom, not this kingdom. Walk with eternity in eyesight; talk with heavenly foresight. Be great in the kingdom of heaven.

Share your experience now at
www.ThirstNoMoreBook.com.

"You have heard that it was said."
—Matthew 5:21

Jesus both affirmed truth and communicated new truth. In His famous Sermon on the Mount, He said, "You have heard that it was said" on multiple occasions to refer to a teaching from the Law of Moses. He affirms "Do not murder" then He furthers this command to extend to anger with another person.

Why this change? Jesus moves beyond the letter of the Law to the spirit of the Law. God stands opposed to murder. But the answer to murder is not simply to "not murder"; the answer is to live in love. To live in anger against another is the first step toward further conflict, the ultimate of which is murder. Jesus commands us to actively pursue peace, not only in the absence of conflict.

Share your experience now at
www.ThirstNoMoreBook.com.

"First go and be reconciled."
—Matthew 5:24

Worship. As followers of Christ, we view offering glory to God as foremost on our spiritual agenda. Yet Jesus places relationship before performance; reconciliation has priority. Before coming to God with our worship, we are to "First go and be reconciled."

These words stand packed with meaning for our lives. "First" stresses the priority of reconciliation. We can rightly stand before God only when we have forgiven others. "Go" demands action. Sometimes we cannot tell ourselves "I forgive her" and move on. Going is necessary. "Be reconciled" is the goal of our action. We do not approach a person we have hurt or who has hurt us to escalate the conflict; we meet to alleviate it. May God show us anyone we need to reconcile with this day.

Share your experience now at
www.ThirstNoMoreBook.com.

"Settle matters quickly with your adversary."
—Matthew 5:25

True spirituality is active, not passive. When in conflict, Christ compels us to reconcile. Further, Christ demands we act quickly. Abraham rose early in the morning when God called Him to offer Isaac as a sacrifice to test his faith. David rose early to worship. Esther fasted immediately to seek God's solution to her plight. God's people move swiftly when conflict is at work.

Rather than seeking to please others, we must seek to please One. In obedience, we are called to work together with those who oppose us for peace. We are commanded to give diligent effort to peacemaking. As we encounter conflict, let us address it quickly. Let us seek His peace each step of our sacred journey.

Share your experience now at
www.ThirstNoMoreBook.com.

FEBRUARY 16

"If your right eye causes you to stumble."
—Matthew 5:29

Gouge out your eyes. Cut off your hand." These are harsh words from the One who has just spoken words of comfort. But a literal mutilation is not His intent. Rather, the focus is the removal of the steps leading to sin. Jesus warns against adultery and the lust that leads to adultery. Both are of concern on His agenda.

We sometimes flippantly walk up to the cliff of sin as closely as possible without falling over the edge. Christ warns us to avoid the edge altogether. We are to turn our eyes in His direction, not the direction of what dishonors Him. Only then will we truly worship. Only then are our hearts clean. Only then can we refrain from stumbling into sin.

Share your experience now at
www.ThirstNoMoreBook.com.

"Anyone who divorces his wife."
—Matthew 5:31

God's view of divorce challenges our contemporary views. Rather than providing ways out, He seeks ways to promote togetherness. Addressing the men in His audience, He taught that any man who divorced his wife, with the exception of infidelity, made his wife the victim of adultery. The husband would be responsible for a grave sin.

Marriage involves a complex range of factors, but Jesus made clear His intent. Some are created for celibacy; others for marriage. Those married are designed for lifelong marriage of man and woman, not a temporary arrangement to fit our selfish interests. We must seek His perspective for our relationships, not our own. Only then do we reflect the way of Jesus and develop families that honor His name.

Share your experience now at
www.ThirstNoMoreBook.com.

"Do not swear an oath at all."
—Matthew 5:34

Can our words be trusted? This is the heart issue addressed here by Jesus. In His culture, people swore by various people, the Temple, or even God. Each appeal strengthened the seriousness of the promise. Jesus rejected this notion entirely. In His words, we are to let our yes be yes and our no be no. Anything else comes from the evil one.

Why? Relationships are built upon trust. If our words cannot be trusted, our relationships are superficial. Only if those around us can count on our commitments will our relationships achieve the depth we desire. Let us reflect on our words today. Are we making promises we cannot keep? Can others trust our words? May God grant us words of truth today.

Share your experience now at
www.ThirstNoMoreBook.com.

"Do not resist an evil person."
—Matthew 5:39

Do not resist an evil person." These words run opposite of everything we have learned as human beings. As children, when someone pushes us, we learn to push back. As adults, when someone wrongs us, our desire is to avenge their injustice. Even God's earlier Law allowed for an eye for an eye, a tooth for a tooth.

"Why live any differently?" is our initial reaction. However, the better question is, "Do I truly wish to live as Jesus did?" Not only did He teach us to live with love toward those who commit injustices toward us, He modeled how to do it. If our goal is to live like Christ, we must increasing fight the urge to avenge those who mistreat us.

Share your experience now at
www.ThirstNoMoreBook.com.

"Love your enemies."
—Matthew 5:44

Enemies exist. There is no use in denying we enjoy some people more than others, whether at the level of preference or due to a person's violence. The Law of Moses taught one to love a neighbor, hate an enemy. Jesus taught to love both neighbor and enemy. There were no exceptions or exemptions. Just "love your enemies."

But how can we love our enemies? Jesus teaches us to pray for them and to love them. This, according to Jesus, is a mark of maturity, not weakness. To love our enemies provides the one weapon they cannot defend against. Injustice cannot overcome love; it can only fight it. In the end, love conquers all. Let us live in love toward those who oppose us today.

Share your experience now at
www.ThirstNoMoreBook.com.

"Pray for those who persecute you."
—Matthew 5:44

Prayer to God is expected; praying for those who persecute us is not. We pray for ourselves, our families, our loved ones. We do not naturally intercede on behalf of those who mock or oppress. Yet Jesus commands us to pray for "those who persecute you."

Praying for those who oppose us does not reflect our self-centered human nature; it reflects God's nature. When we pray for our enemies, we are "children of your Father in heaven." We have become like our Daddy, One who loves every person He has created unconditionally. Such prayers are not only to change our enemies, but to change our hearts. When we ask God to transform those who oppose us, we are also asking God to transform us.

Share your experience now at
www.ThirstNoMoreBook.com.

"Be perfect . . . as your heavenly Father is perfect."
—Matthew 5:48

We are imperfect people. Yet Jesus commands us to "be perfect." How is this possible? The word translated "be perfect" can also be translated "mature" or "complete." We can never reach perfection in this life, but we can become mature.

Jesus even communicates how to become spiritually mature. It includes caring about those who do not care about us. We are called to love and pray for those who oppose our values. Christ commands us to love those who hate us; to show life to those who wish to take our lives. Our true test of belief is not how we respond among God's people, but how we reflect God among those who are not His people. Show love. Pray. Become mature. "Be perfect."

Share your experience now at
www.ThirstNoMoreBook.com.

"Be careful...in front of others."
—Matthew 6:1

Helping others wins applause. This is one reason every religion and political party champions the cause of the poor and others in need. When we look good, the perception is that we are good.

Jesus knew of this temptation. He had been pressured by Satan in the wilderness to perform for the crowds. He resisted. Further, He taught to be careful not to give to the needy so others can see. We give to those in need and God sees. There is not necessarily a command to secrecy, but there is a command to priority. Our goal must be to receive God's honor, not the crowd's honor. He is the One we must seek to worship; His applause is all that ultimately matters.

Share your experience now at
www.ThirstNoMoreBook.com.

"When you pray."
—Matthew 6:5

Prayer is not optional for followers of Christ. His teaching on prayer presumes praying takes place regularly and proceeds with instructions regarding how to pray. In the time of Jesus, religious leaders often sought to pray in public venues for attention. Whether standing in their local synagogue on the Sabbath or a street corner during the week, prayer was not passionate intercession but rather public relations.

Authentic prayer is conversation with God. As such, we should desire to pray in an uninterrupted environment far from the crowds. Though public prayer has its place, extended, contemplative prayer requires extended solitude in God's presence. If we are struggling to hear clearly from God, perhaps a new time and place for communing with our Lord is required.

Share your experience now at
www.ThirstNoMoreBook.com.

"Do not be like the hypocrites."
—Matthew 6:5

Who is a hypocrite? According to Jesus, a hypocrite includes someone who does spiritual things to be seen by others. Based on this definition, this could include church leaders, celebrities, or ourselves. The corrective is not to end praying in public, however. The solution lies in a vibrant personal prayer life far from the noise of the crowd.

Spiritual leaders such as Moses, David, and Daniel spoke of extended times of quiet prayer before the Lord. God used these people to lead others not because of their human abilities, but their spiritual availability. Though they were ultimately imperfect servants serving a holy God, He used them in part due to their deep, abiding prayer with Him. As they have done, so we must do.

Share your experience now at
www.ThirstNoMoreBook.com.

*"Your Father knows what you need
before you ask him."*
—Matthew 6:8

God does not need our prayers; we need our prayers. Our Father knows our thoughts before we think them; He knows our requests before they are requested. Why, then, do we pray at all?

We pray to commune with God. If we love someone, we will spend time with that person. God is no exception. If we truly love Him, we will long for extended times to interact. No one should need to remind us to pray any more than someone should remind us to love our children or our spouse. Those we love, we long to see; for in connecting, our love grows, our relationship deepens. Let us seek time with our Lord today. Let us run to Him, our Friend, Redeemer, and Savior.

Share your experience now at
www.ThirstNoMoreBook.com.

"This, then, is how you should pray."
—Matthew 6:9

Jesus makes clear there is a method to prayer. Just as a letter includes a form and a model follows instructions, prayer includes a pattern. In the Lord's Prayer, Jesus provides the criteria necessary for meaningfully addressing God.

Yet it is critical we realize there is a deep connection between our attitude of prayer and the content of our prayer. In the preceding words, Jesus spoke of the necessary manner in which we should approach the Father. In the following words, Jesus highlights the values and principles essential to communicating with our Creator. Both are essential, a proper attitude and appropriate words. May the Lord grant us both in our time with Him today. May He be pleased with our consciences and our communications.

Share your experience now at
www.ThirstNoMoreBook.com.

"Our Father in heaven."
–Matthew 6:9

Our. Father. In. Heaven. These four opening words to the Lord's Prayer communicate both depth and sacredness. "Our" highlights God as Father of every person who trusts God in childlike faith. "Father" displays His relationship as our loving leader, both above us and connected with us in way beyond the capacity for language to express.

"In" provides a significant note regarding place. God exists in all places at all times, yet His glory stretches beyond our known experience to the heavenly realms. "Heaven" could refer to the skies, but also indicates God is wholly other, existing in a capacity unique to Him. We would do well to remember the weight of Christ's words today: "Our Father in heaven."

Share your experience now at
www.ThirstNoMoreBook.com.

"Hallowed be your name."
—Matthew 6:9

Hallowed" communicates the idea of holy, set apart. God is our Friend, but He is foremost our Father. To approach God requires an acknowledgement of His power and our frailty. It has been said our lives are dominated by our view of God. If we view God as a benevolent grandfather, we will pray weak prayer and live life in our own power. If we view God as Creator and Sustainer of all life, Rescuer from sin, we will pray in profound intercessions, bowed in humility before the Lord Almighty.

We likely know God is holy, yet we can also easily forget His majesty. If our prayers feel weak, one of the best responses is the reminder of God's holiness, His power, His greatness.

Share your experience now at
www.ThirstNoMoreBook.com.

MARCH 1

"Your kingdom come."
—Matthew 6:10

We each live as citizens a nation. Yet as followers of Jesus we are also citizens of another kingdom—the kingdom of God. It already exists, though we do not yet see it. One day, all those who belong to Christ will live in this eternal kingdom with Christ Himself as King.

This future kingdom is the emphasis behind praying "Your kingdom come." We are not asking for a change of government; we are asking for the final return of Christ. When He returns, injustice will cease; pain will end; sin will be no more. There will be no tears, no sorrow; only joy. When we pray, let us ask God "Your kingdom come." One day it will and we will see Him face-to-face.

Share your experience now at
www.ThirstNoMoreBook.com.

MARCH 2

"Your will be done."
—Matthew 6:10

Selfish prayers come easily. Perhaps that is why Jesus chooses to include in the early portion of the Lord's Prayer, "Your will be done." To select "Your will" as one of the first requests we offer our Creator, we acknowledge both His greatness and our willingness to submit to His authority.

Anyone can pray "give me" prayers. "God, grant me wisdom," "Give me health," "Give me a better job." To pray "Your will be done" requires a certain level of humility and maturity obtained through a high view of God and His ways. As we pray, let us not look first to our needs or even the requests of others. Let us before all else ask our Father "Your will be done."

Share your experience now at
www.ThirstNoMoreBook.com.

"On earth as it is in heaven."
—Matthew 6:10

Collision. When we pray for God's will on earth as in heaven, we are asking for nothing less than a collision between heaven and earth, God's perfection and our world's imperfections. In heaven, God's will is the pleasure of His servants. There is no sin there; therefore, God's desires are completely fulfilled.

On earth, God's will also comes to pass, but due to sin, much takes place that saddens His heart. To ask "on earth as it is in heaven" intercedes for our Father to remove barriers and accomplish His desires in our lives and the lives of others. The danger of this petition is that He chooses to use us to answer this prayer. May we prepare our spirits to live out His desires today.

Share your experience now at
www.ThirstNoMoreBook.com.

"Give us today our daily bread."
—Matthew 6:11

The Lord's Prayer challenges us in these words perhaps more than any other portion. Countless "experts" teach us to strategically plan our days, provide vision, and work to advance the kingdom. The words of Jesus simply focus on today: "Give us today our daily bread."

There is no request for next week's food or even for tomorrow's meal. Our request is on the need of the moment. In a culture where preparing a meal could take a full day, this petition offered focus. Let us focus today not on the problems of next year or even next week; let us focus our hearts to God on today's rigors; let our souls live fully attuned to His provision for our daily needs.

Share your experience now at
www.ThirstNoMoreBook.com.

"And forgive us our debts."
—Matthew 6:12

Forgiveness lives at the heart of true Christianity. No other religious system offers such complete removal of sin and new life. Yet those of us who approach the Father are asked to incorporate in our prayers to ask for forgiveness: "forgive us our debts."

Why pray for forgiveness when we have already been forgiven? If we follow the risen Christ, our sins are no more. Yet our sins are called "debts," indicating our need for "credit" from God. Without His removal of our debts, we remain stained by the daily impact of our human failings. Such understanding is essential to spiritual growth; such acknowledgement is required for the humility God seeks. Let us ask Him for forgiveness; let us walk in newness of life.

Share your experience now at
www.ThirstNoMoreBook.com.

"As we have forgiven our debtors."
—Matthew 6:12

In the Lord's Prayer lies only one conditional request: forgive us as we have forgiven others. Why forgiveness? Doesn't our Father forgive unconditionally? He does, yet these words reveal God's mercy is somehow intricately connected with the mercy we show to others.

Is there a person in our lives we refuse to forgive? If so, this weakens our prayers. In some enigmatic way, unforgiveness presents a barrier to our intimacy with God. As such, any lack of forgiveness on our part cannot be delayed. We are compelled to confront our bitterness immediately. God strengthen us to forgive those who have hurt us. May we forgive our debtors as you have forgiven our debts. Let us remove any barrier that separates us from intimacy with You.

Share your experience now at
www.ThirstNoMoreBook.com.

"Lead us not into temptation."
—Matthew 6:13

Temptation. Even Christ was tempted by the devil. Three times He resisted, speaking God's Word in His defense. In the Lord's Prayer, Jesus instructs His listeners to ask God not to lead us into temptation. Why? Temptation is the first step toward sin.

Temptation is not sin; submitting to temptation is sin. Yet instead of asking for strength to resist temptation, the Lord's Prayer addresses temptation itself. This offers a tremendous insight for us in breaking free from sin. When an area of weakness dominates, the answer may be to pray for the temptation leading to the sin to be removed. May God help us confront the flaws in our lives, seeking His solutions to our frailty.

Share your experience now at
www.ThirstNoMoreBook.com.

"Deliver us from the evil one."
—Matthew 6:13

Jesus had been "delivered" from Satan. After His three temptations, the devil left Him. Here He instructs His listeners to pray for God's rescue from the evil one. Why? First, we need God to answer because Satan does have great spiritual power. He deceives, lies, and twists the truth. Apart from God's intervention, we are helpless against the evil one.

Second, we know God has power over Satan. Jesus proved this in His resistance to temptation. In these words, He calls us to rely on God's power. Evil exists and is strong, but not compared to God. Connected to God's strength, the evil one has no authority over us. We can rest assured in God's hands that He will "deliver us from the evil one."

Share your experience now at
www.ThirstNoMoreBook.com.

"If you forgive other people."
—Matthew 6:14

It is easier to ask God for forgiveness than for us to forgive others. Perhaps this why Jesus mentions this as a condition of God's mercy toward us. Some have suggested that only in forgiving others do we prove we ourselves have been forgiven. Regardless of the specific correlation between our forgiveness and God's, there is no doubt the two cannot be separated.

God grants forgiveness; He also expects forgiveness. When we fail to extend grace to those who have hurt us, we reveal we have yet to understand His forgiveness as we ought. Only in giving up our vengeance toward those who have sinned against us do we display the majesty of God's love toward our own souls—a love amazing, deep, divine.

Share your experience now at
www.ThirstNoMoreBook.com.

"When you fast."
—Matthew 6:16

To fast is to set aside time to go without food to focus on God. Even prior to the early Christian church, God's people fasted on occasion in devotion to the Lord. This practice was expected: "When you fast," not "If you fast."

In our culture, food dominates discussion and schedules. To go without food represents one agreed-to pause to our hectic lives. Yet this is precisely what Christ desires—to be Lord of all, not Lord of part. Fasting concentrates our attention on Him in a unique way. Our hunger is about Him, for Him, because of Him. If you have not fasted, consider what it would take to begin. If your health allows, go without to hear from God. He will answer "when you fast."

Share your experience now at
www.ThirstNoMoreBook.com.

"Do not store up for yourselves treasures on earth."
—Matthew 6:19

There is a very real temptation to make the pursuit of financial gain priority one. Yet Jesus makes clear this is not His priority for us. Money is fleeting; possessions are temporary. The one whose eyes are fixed on eternity will not see money as a prize, but only as a tool to achieve the purposes of God.

Many wealthy individuals come to the end of life with much regret. They realize too late, money could not accomplish the joy they sought. True joy is found in the Lord. Our possessions are a gift from God, but God is the gift. May our journey this day focus on the Giver of our treasures and not the treasures themselves. May we seek Him above all else.

Share your experience now at
www.ThirstNoMoreBook.com.

"Store up for yourselves treasures in heaven."
—Matthew 6:20

What are treasures in heaven? We are not given full details, but some observations can be ascertained. First, heavenly treasures are contrasted with earthly treasures. Treasures in heaven include a focus on what lasts, what is eternal, what matters most.

Scripture also reveals there are spiritual rewards to be given to God's people in eternity future. These will be based on the lives we live now. We are to pursue full devotion to our Father that we may hear Him say, "Well done, my good and faithful servant." If we do, we need not worry about the specific nature of our heavenly treasure. God will handle the accounting! Most importantly, we will be with Him, the greatest imaginable treasure of all.

Share your experience now at
www.ThirstNoMoreBook.com.

*"Where your treasure is,
there your heart will be also."*
—Matthew 6:21

Jesus specifies two treasures—treasures on earth and those in heaven. He concludes that our heart will be where our treasure is. We cannot pursue both worldly success and eternal success at the same time. One contradicts the other. We will constantly compromise either to Christ or the crowd. We cannot always please both.

Our Lord mentions this so we would choose wisely. Will we choose success in the eyes of others? Is the attention of our peers, our family, or even thousands of fans enough to satisfy? Or is there a discontent with worldly pleasure? If so, our answer lies in treasure in heaven. When we seek eternal realities, we find true joy. If our treasure is in Christ, our hearts will be fixed on Him.

Share your experience now at
www.ThirstNoMoreBook.com.

"The eye is the lamp of the body."
—Matthew 6:22

A lamp in the ancient world gave light to a room or along a path. If the lamp were bright, the whole room would be filled with light. If the lamp was of poor quality, little could be seen; progress would be stifled.

Jesus uses this analogy to teach the importance of our focus. If focused on the wrong priorities, our lives will follow those priorities, leaving a path displeasing to God. If focused on the right priority, the pursuit of Christ's ways, our life will likewise follow. The importance of our priorities cannot be overstated. If Christ is preeminent in all things, our lives will reflect His love; our souls will be full of light. Place Jesus above all else today.

Share your experience now at
www.ThirstNoMoreBook.com.

"No one can serve two masters."
—Matthew 6:24

Have you ever worked a job with two bosses? Were you ever able to please both of them for long? Of course not! To fully please a leader requires total loyalty and devotion. Jesus highlights this from a spiritual perspective. As He teaches about God and money, He notes we cannot serve both. We must choose.

Whether in money or the pleasures money can buy, we must live very sensitively to the danger of serving the master of self over our Savior. Money offers buying power; only God can offer spiritual power. Unless we give our full allegiance to Christ, He is not our Master. No one can serve two masters. Only one can be first. Let us choose to follow our Master Jesus.

Share your experience now at
www.ThirstNoMoreBook.com.

"Do not worry about your life."
—Matthew 6:25

Worry can paralyze. With difficult choices and limited time, our human inclination is to fret over the various scenarios that lie ahead. Jesus teaches a different perspective. As God, He created all things, utilizing an unfathomable combination of options to hang the sun, moon, and stars in place. Yet such effort did not strain Him. His power is endless, unbounded by our limitations.

We are not to worry about our lives, because the same One who created the universe lives within us who believe in the Son. Our humanity has limits; our God does not. He knows what we need before we do. His answer is already on the way. To worry casts doubt on His ability. To trust acknowledges faith in His power.

Share your experience now at
www.ThirstNoMoreBook.com.

"Seek first his kingdom and his righteousness."
—Matthew 6:33

The alternative to not worrying is to seek first God's kingdom and righteousness. This sounds strangely vague on the surface. However, Jesus did not seek to confuse us. His listeners understood Jesus again referred to a view toward eternity and a focus on sacred living. These two traits stand powerfully and intricately connected.

To seek God's kingdom is to long for eternity— whether through Christ's return or our departure from this world to live with Him forever. To seek His righteousness is to pursue a life pleasing to God now. Both are essential for those of us wish to escape worry. In fact, both are essential for those of us who wish to truly worship. Let us look toward eternity and live in light of this reality this day.

Share your experience now at
www.ThirstNoMoreBook.com.

"Do not judge, or you too will be judged."
—Matthew 7:1

Our culture embraces a skewed view of judgment. We seek freedom from all condemnation, freedom to live as we wish. All views are granted equality. Every opinion is blessed with importance. It is only expected then that many would apply this attitude toward God, embracing "Do not judge" without qualification.

Jesus taught not to judge, or we would be judged. He next claims we will be judged to the same degree we judge others. Nowhere is condemning sin excluded; only to do so after self-evaluation. We are called to help others. Yet we cannot expect to speak with credibility without first unmasking our own sins. Let us remove the plank from our own eyes that we may help others remove the specks from their own.

Share your experience now at
www.ThirstNoMoreBook.com.

"Seek and you will find."
—Matthew 7:7

A loving Father desires to provide good gifts. In fact, a loving parent will often surprise a child with a special gift that has been requested. The asking makes the receiving even more special: *You remembered! You cared enough give what I wanted.*

Granted, God does not give us everything we want, just as a wise parent does not grant a child every request. But God does enjoy surprising us with many of the gifts we desire. He calls for us to ask, to seek. When we do, He provides, bringing joy to us and to the heart of God. "Seek and you will find" is not just about us; it is about the relationship between the heart of a loving Father and his children.

Share your experience now at
www.ThirstNoMoreBook.com.

"Do to others as you would have them do to you."
—Matthew 7:12

How do we like to be treated? With respect, dignity, love. Jesus knew this. Perhaps this is precisely why He taught us to treat others as we would have them treat us. He knew to apply this statement would require an abrupt change in how we naturally prefer to treat those we meet.

Our natural response is to treat others as if they existed for our pleasure. We wish to stand on the receiving end of "customer service": the customer is always right. But Jesus flipped the equation into a situation where we are the servants, not the recipients. We are called to serve others rather than demand service from others. Only then do we reflect Christ, the One who gave His life for us.

Share your experience now at
www.ThirstNoMoreBook.com.

MARCH 21

"Enter through the narrow gate."
—Matthew 7:13

What is the narrow gate? Clearly, a narrow gate would be more difficult to enter than a wide gate or a wide road. The indication here is that Jesus teaches His way is limited; His path is hard. In fact, Jesus taught "only a few find it."

Rather than promising the way of Jesus is easy or everyone spends eternity with Him, He made clear—not everyone will follow. Instead, He challenges listeners to enter the narrow gate; to take on the more difficult task of finding His way regardless of the risk. Jesus is the way, not a way. To serve Him requires struggle, devotion, and commitment. Let us rise to the challenge of entering His narrow gate today.

Share your experience now at
www.ThirstNoMoreBook.com.

"Every good tree bears good fruit."
—Matthew 7:17

The quality of a fruit tree is evident to those who know how to spot one. Despite the beauty of its leaves or size of its branches, the trained observer can declare a tree good or bad based on an examination of its fruit.

Jesus compares His followers to trees. Despite our size or external qualities, what matters is our fruit. Deceiving teachers can imitate the look and feel of a true disciple, but they cannot copy our fruit. This is why Jesus taught, "By their fruit you will recognize them." We need not join them, but rather must develop the fruit of God's Spirit. Let us live that others may see us flourishing as trees in the garden of the King.

Share your experience now at
www.ThirstNoMoreBook.com.

"Not everyone"
—Matthew 7:21

Many neglect the hard words of Jesus, living as if they do not stand between the prayers and healings in the Gospels. Yet Jesus spoke difficult truth at times. In fact, He claimed, "Not everyone who says to me, 'Lord, Lord,' will enter the kingdom of heaven." Something more is required than calling on His name.

In fact, even some who prophesy and send away demons will not enter heaven. Only those who do the will of the Father enter the kingdom. What is this "will"? To believe in the Son. Anything less will miss eternity with God, regardless of one's efforts. Let us bow in worship at the provision of God's Son, Jesus, today. Let us live with passion to share His love.

Share your experience now at
www.ThirstNoMoreBook.com.

"Like a wise man."
—Matthew 7:24

The story of the wise man and foolish man in the Gospels has often been misapplied. The emphasis typically falls on the importance of the planning skills of the wise man. The error to avoid is the improper preparation of the foolish man.

But Jesus used these two types of men to highlight a different message. He taught that those who heard His words and put them into action resembled the wise man. The focus is on the application of what Jesus had taught. His story stood as the conclusion of His Sermon on the Mount, a rally cry for action rather than mere reaction. May God make us like the true "wise man," living as people who hear and obey the words of Jesus.

Share your experience now at
www.ThirstNoMoreBook.com.

"The crowds were amazed at his teaching."
—Matthew 7:28

When Jesus taught, people listened. In fact, His hearers were "amazed at his teaching." Why? His authority. In contrast with their religious teachers, Jesus spoke the words of God. His power stood out above the other lecturers of their time.

Even today many are amazed at the teachings of Jesus. Some find them fascinating; others, empowering. When we hear from Jesus, we tend to know there is a power beyond ourselves, an authority above our own. This very detail highlights the importance of God's enduring Word for our lives today. If we wish to hear from God, we need not look far. We must only turn to the teaching of His Word. There we will find instruction and be—just as His original audience—amazed.

Share your experience now at
www.ThirstNoMoreBook.com.

"You can make me clean."
—Matthew 8:2

A crowd had surrounded Jesus. One man braved the audience to kneel before the Rabbi. His request? "Lord, if you are willing, you can make me clean." His petition offers three essential insights for our times in God's presence.

First, this diseased man addressed Jesus as "Lord." He rightly acknowledged Jesus as the Anointed One, the Christ. Second, he sought God's will before his own: "If you are willing." Third, this kneeling individual understood Christ's healing power: "You can make me clean." We, likewise, do well to come to Jesus as Lord, seek His will before our own, and bow before His power. Jesus healed this man; He, too, can heal the pains of our lives today. Jesus can make us clean.

Share your experience now at
www.ThirstNoMoreBook.com.

"Lord, I do not deserve."
—Matthew 8:8

Not many people amazed Jesus during His time on earth. A certain Roman leader stood as an exception. This centurion came to Jesus and asked for healing upon his servant. Jesus then asked what would become a profound question, "Shall I come and heal him?"

The centurion answered, "Lord, I do not deserve to have you come under my roof." Jesus was amazed. Earlier, the crowds stood amazed by His teaching. Here, Jesus stood amazed at the centurion's faith. In response, Jesus declared the servant healed. The physical healing took place at the exact time Jesus spoke. A life was changed by one person's faith. It began with humility. May we live as this centurion, praying, "Lord, I do not deserve."

Share your experience now at
www.ThirstNoMoreBook.com.

"He took up our infirmities."
—Matthew 8:17

choing the prophet Isaiah, Matthew noted Jesus was the Messiah because "He took up our infirmities." Jesus did not come to earth only to identify with our frail humanity; He came to heal it. What began with healing the mother-in-law of Peter extended to many who came to this Rabbi-Healer.

Jesus could remove demons and disease; nothing stood beyond His power. As people recognized His ability, they shared stories, resulting in many coming to Him. We, too, experience the power of Christ healing both physically and spiritually. We, as those of old, must share these stories. As we do, others will come to Him—and believe. Jesus holds power over sickness and spiritual oppression. He alone holds the power to transform body and spirit.

Share your experience now at
www.ThirstNoMoreBook.com.

"The Son of Man has no place to lay his head."
—Matthew 8:20

Many overlook the detail that Jesus was homeless. He did not only teach the poor; He lived among them. Jesus was a king by identity; He became homeless to identify. Those who sought to follow Him were at times turned off by this lifestyle, as many are today. Many desire a "calling" for Jesus, a job with benefits. Others seek a role convenient with their family situation.

Jesus was not antiwork or antifamily, but He pointed out an essential conviction—following Christ is costly. We are not given permission to take a holiday from discipleship, nor can we choose when to serve or where. Our relationship stands as a servant to master; our only proper response is, "I will follow You."

Share your experience now at
www.ThirstNoMoreBook.com.

"You of little faith."
—Matthew 8:26

When disaster strikes, we instinctively cry out to God. Whether airplane turbulence or a car headed toward our headlights, "Lord, save me!" often escapes our lips. The same was true of the disciples. A fierce storm attacked their boat. Death became a grim reality. In their moment of crisis, however, Jesus slept! They interrupted His slumber, shouting, "Save us! We're going to drown!"

Jesus knew what would happen. He used the scenario as an object lesson. "You of little faith, why are you so afraid?" They feared drowning; their phobia was death. Jesus called their fear a lack of faith. In our fear, we must recall Christ is with us; we need not panic. He is with us in the boat. Lord, increase our faith!

Share your experience now at
www.ThirstNoMoreBook.com.

"What kind of man is this?"
—Matthew 8:27

After the Resurrection, the disciples would refer to Jesus as Messiah. Here, He is referred to as a man. Jesus stopped the storm, controlling the very powers of nature. They had seen healings, but never such power. "What kind of man is this?"

They would soon discover this man was the God-Man. Still today, those who experience Jesus or study His life often ask, "What kind of man is this?" The answer is that He was never only a man; He was and is the Messiah, the Creator of wind and waves. He controls and sustains life. He offers eternal and abundant life. May we stand in awe of Him once again. May we continually live in amazement at the power of our risen Christ.

Share your experience now at
www.ThirstNoMoreBook.com.

"The demons begged Jesus."
—Matthew 8:31

People often fear, or are fascinated by, the supernatural. Experiencing the unseen casts a strange thrill—one many believe they should seek. Jesus sheds light on this invisible world as two demon-possessed men approach him on the shore of Gadarenes. These demons ask, "What do you want with us?"; "Have you come to torture us?"; and "Send us into the herd of pigs."

These demons even called Jesus the Son of God. Spiritual forces of evil know who Jesus is and the power He has. They fear Him. In our human strength, the demonic realm poses fear. In Christ, we walk in faith; spirits tremble at His name. In Christ, we need not fear nor be fascinated by the supernatural. Jesus holds authority over darkness.

Share your experience now at
www.www.ThirstNoMoreBook.com.

APRIL 2

"When Jesus saw their faith."
—Matthew 9:2

Jesus attracted many who desired healing. But what about those who could not reach Him on their own? This was the predicament of one paralyzed man. He had no access to Jesus; no ability to connect. His prospects for claiming Christ's healing power stood at zero.

But not if the paralyzed man had help. We are told "some men" brought this person to Jesus, carrying him on a mat. Alone, he had no chance. With the help of others, he laid at the foot of Jesus. This same powerful principle applies still today. Alone many have little chance of finding Christ; through you, they could get to Jesus Himself, ready to receive forgiveness and healing. Bring someone who is hurting into the presence of Jesus.

Share your experience now at
www.ThirstNoMoreBook.com.

"Your sins are forgiven."
—Matthew 9:2

Jesus had become known as a healer. Crowds flocked to Him in every town. Yet something different happened when a certain paralyzed man was brought before Him. Rather than declare him healed, Jesus chose to say, "Take heart, son; your sins are forgiven."

The religious leaders claimed Jesus had committed blasphemy. "Who can forgive sin but God?" was on their mind. This was exactly the point Jesus sought to make. He had power over the body and over the soul. Leaders in the past had provided healing, but no one had granted forgiveness. Jesus made His authority clear. The question is whether we will submit to His power or walk in our own strength. Let us live by His might this day.

Share your experience now at
www.ThirstNoMoreBook.com.

"Follow me."
—Matthew 9:9

Matthew may have had the most despised background of any disciple. He also claims the record for the shortest call from Jesus: "Follow me." With just two words, one sinner was changed forever. Matthew immediately left his government role to follow the leader of One whose kingdom was not of this world.

Many have speculated what caused Matthew to join Jesus with only a two-word challenge. There is no clear answer, but what is clear is that Matthew heard the voice of Christ and responded. Such conviction challenges our conventions. Sometimes we don't need confirming signs or external evidence; we need simply to listen to Christ—and obey. Regardless of our background, He will use us for His pleasure, changing us and through us, changing others.

Share your experience now at
www.ThirstNoMoreBook.com.

"It is not the healthy who need a doctor."
—Matthew 9:12

Jesus joined a dinner party with Matthew and many others. This crew must have included some notorious locals, as local religious teachers confronted Christ's disciples in protest. "Why does your teacher eat with tax collectors and sinners?" they asked. When Jesus heard of it, He addressed their question directly. "It is not the healthy who need a doctor, but the sick."

What did Jesus mean? Simply that His mission was intended for those in need of mercy. In fact, Jesus challenged His inquisitors to find the meaning behind the statement, "I desire mercy, not sacrifice." His goal was never to fit in comfortably with the religious leaders of His time. His purpose was to save sinners, to show mercy, to extend grace. May we live the same.

Share your experience now at
www.ThirstNoMoreBook.com.

"Then they will fast."
—Matthew 9:15

John's disciples were curious folks. Looking to Jesus and His followers, they noticed there was no practice of fasting or abstaining from food. When they asked Him about it, Jesus did not deny the importance of this practice. Instead, He noted the timing was not right.

Timing is critical to many aspects of our spirituality. The writer of Ecclesiastes also taught there was a time for everything—a time to weep, a time for joy; a time to sow, a time to reap. We often think our time is best for whatever spiritual change we wish to make, but the Lord has His own schedule. When we seek His direction, we may find answers unpopular to ourselves or others, but must trust His timing is best.

Share your experience now at
www.ThirstNoMoreBook.com.

"If I only touch His cloak."
—Matthew 9:21

Despite His healing powers, many skeptics doubted Jesus. Neither the top religious teachers nor the leading government had endorsed His efforts. Yet one diseased woman believed otherwise. In faith, she believed, "If I only touch His cloak, I will be healed." Despite the doubters, the vast crowd, and her physical condition, she made her way step by painful step to this young rabbi.

After several agonizing attempts, she finally stretched out and touched His garment. At her touch, Jesus turned, speaking words she would never forget: "Take heart, daughter…your faith has healed you." Her 12 years of pain instantly disappeared. She was healed. We, too, stand in need of healing in many ways. Perhaps Jesus is simply waiting for us to reach out in faith…to touch Him.

Share your experience now at
www.ThirstNoMoreBook.com.

"The girl is not dead but asleep."
—Matthew 9:24

Leaders are powerful people. Through their appearance and influence, celebrities attract attention and perform actions beyond the norm. Jesus had recently started attracting buzz at the level of a leader or even a celebrity. Through His healings and speeches, many had heard of the healing rabbi who spoke with authority.

But no one expected what was about to happen. Except one. One dad, in desperation, sought Jesus on behalf of his daughter. Devastated, he suggested, "My daughter has just died. But come and put your hand on her, and she will live." Jesus did go; He did take her by the hand; she did live. When others doubt the power of Jesus, be the one who asks Him to perform the impossible. He often will.

Share your experience now at
www.ThirstNoMoreBook.com.

APRIL 9

"Have mercy on us."
—Matthew 9:27

As Jesus walked along, two blind men approached Him. We do not know how they reached Him or identified Him. What we are given is their plea: "Have mercy on us, Son of David!" Taking them aside, Jesus asked one question, "Do you believe I am able to do this?" They replied, "Yes." He gave them sight.

Their example communicates volumes. Are we willing to throw ourselves before Christ, declaring, "Have mercy"? Do we acknowledge Him as the "Son of David," the Messiah who was to come? Do we believe He can provide vision for our lives? If so, we can expect Jesus to act on our behalf. He will transform us. He will grant us the ability to see things rightly.

Share your experience now at
www.ThirstNoMoreBook.com.

"Nothing like this has ever been seen."
—Matthew 9:33

After sending away yet another evil spirit from a man, two responses emerged from the crowd. The first, claimed among the common people, noted, "Nothing like this has ever been seen." The second view came from the religious teachers. They claimed His power over demons came from Satan himself.

When the supernatural occurs, these two views continue to dominate. Some stand in awe; others seek alternative explanations. Even among those who believe, it is often easier to cast doubt than stand in awe when God is at work. Rather than reflect the view of those who rejected Christ, we must seek to remain in awe at His power and actions. Jesus, as God's Son, is supernatural. He is our all-powerful, awe-inspiring Savior.

Share your experience now at
www.ThirstNoMoreBook.com.

"He had compassion on them."
—Matthew 9:36

Jesus is full of compassion. When He experienced the needs of people, He cared. Rather than a distant deity, Jesus lived among us as a caring friend. He saw people as sheep without a shepherd.

The imagery of sheep would have been common among His audience. Sheep required leadership. On their own, sheep had little hope for survival against enemies or the elements. They stood weak and helpless. Likewise, Jesus saw the crowds of His day in need of leaders to point them to the Father. He asked His followers to pray for workers for the harvest, noting the laborers are few. May we live and lead others to be such laborers. May we live with the compassion of our Christ.

Share your experience now at
www.ThirstNoMoreBook.com.

"Jesus called his twelve disciples to him."
—Matthew 10:1

Jesus never intended to operate solo. From the beginning, He called others not only to follow Him, but to serve alongside Him. What was His approach? First, He selected a small group of followers to join Him. In contrast with the widening crowds, Jesus invested the majority of His time into the cluster of influencers who would multiply His legacy among others.

Second, He sent others out under His authority. Christ not only provided errands to run, He offered on-the-job experience. The Twelve cast out demons, healed the sick, and declared, "The kingdom of heaven has come near." They repeated what Jesus had started from their first day with Him. Jesus continues to challenge us both to follow Him and further His cause.

Share your experience now at
www.ThirstNoMoreBook.com.

"Be on your guard."
—Matthew 10:17

Christianity is anything but safe. Jesus made clear trouble and persecution stood in the future of His followers. They would be flogged, taken before the courts; later, most of the disciples would be killed for their faith. He had saved them, but not for safety; He saved them for service.

We often deny or downplay this reality. Persecution is expected for those who follow Christ. In fact, if we are not receiving some type of ridicule for our beliefs, we are probably doing something wrong. The apostle Paul noted, "Everyone who wants to live a godly life in Christ Jesus will be persecuted" (2 Timothy 3:12). Jesus promised peace in eternity, not on earth. We must prepare to suffer; living for Christ despite any consequences.

Share your experience now at
www.ThirstNoMoreBook.com.

April 14

"Whoever loses their life for my sake will find it."
—Matthew 10:39

The key to finding life in Christ is in losing our lives in Him. Jesus made clear His conviction that He must come ahead of parents, son, or daughter. No one can have more influence in our lives than Him. In fact, we are commanded to take up our cross and follow Him, a symbol of death and torture.

If we fail to place Jesus first, we are not worthy of Him. This is not an arrogant statement, but rather a statement of fact. If Jesus is not foremost in our lives, He is simply not God to us. Something else is. Only when we abandon other pursuits to the degree they fall below our allegiance to Him are we truly serving Him as king.

Share your experience now at
www.ThirstNoMoreBook.com.

"Even a cup of cold water."
—Matthew 10:42

Jesus rejoices in even the smallest gifts to His children. A cold cup of water given to one of His disciples in His name leads to an eternal reward. Yet how often we miss this! We seek fame, the largest circle of influence possible, the most strategic location. Yet size, speed, nor influence is Christ's system of measurement—love is.

Since God is love, He measures our lives by our love. Can we look to our past day or even past year in this manner and find ourselves faithful? In some ways, yes; yet with this standard of measurement there is much room for improvement. Our goal cannot be to "be better" than our neighbor. Our goal is one cup of water at a time.

Share your experience now at
www.ThirstNoMoreBook.com.

"Are you the one who is to come."
—Matthew 11:3

John, in prison, certainly had his doubts. One was to confirm whether Jesus was the Messiah. He would soon die for this belief; he wanted to be sure his death was not in vain. John's followers asked on his behalf, "Are you the one who is to come?"

Jesus answered brilliantly: "Report to John what you hear and see." What were these reports? The blind received sight; the sick, healed; the dead, raised to life. John should have no doubt. Jesus was the Messiah. We, too, doubt at times. Yet Christ's deeds are greater than our doubt. We need only be reminded of what He has done to remember who He truly is. He is the One who was to come.

Share your experience now at
www.ThirstNoMoreBook.com.

"You have hidden these things from the wise."
—Matthew 11:25

Those wise in this world often miss the message of Christ. Why is this? When people trust in their own wisdom, they no longer listen to the wisdom of others. This is especially true regarding faith issues–areas requiring "less wisdom" than our human limitations are often willing to accept.

Jesus, however, praised the Father for hiding His message from the wise and revealing it to "little children." Only when we come to God in child-like faith can we accept His message, regardless of our human capacities. If we wish for God to reveal Himself to us, we must be willing to humble ourselves as His children. Anything less misses His true message, His deepest revelation. Are we willing to come as little children?

Share your experience now at
www.ThirstNoMoreBook.com.

"Come to me,
all you who are weary and burdened."
—Matthew 11:28

Weary" and "burdened" are not words we often mention in daily conversation. When asked, "How are you doing?" we answer, "I'm keeping busy." Our culture values the rush of life, not reflection; action, not weakness; pursuits of the moment, not lasting peace.

God's view of our lives is far different. He sees our troubles. He knows our struggles. And He still longs for us to come. Our all-powerful Creator stands aware of our imperfections. Still, this does not stop His interest in sharing time with us. In contrast, He embraces us at our point of helplessness and provides what is lacking to help us continue our daily pursuits. If we find ourselves weary today, we need only to answer His call— "Come to me."

Share your experience now at
www.ThirstNoMoreBook.com.

APRIL 19

"I will give you rest."
—Matthew 11:28

We commonly associate rest with sleep. Sleep creates a reserve of energy, but it is not the source of our replenishment. True rest comes from God alone. Only He can offer something beyond physical restoration, a supernatural focus matched to our exact daily encounters.

Christ's first disciples learned directly from their Rabbi Jesus who offers lasting rest. Rest is not a level of energy, restraint from activity, or escape from reality. Rest is to come to the One who controls every particle in the universe, the One who provides everything we need for life and godliness. We are called to come to Him. Jesus will give us rest. In Him, we live and move and have our being.

Share your experience now at
www.ThirstNoMoreBook.com.

"You will find rest."
—Matthew 11:29

Rest is often a missing reality in our lives. There is always another task, another conversation, another place to consume our time. Perhaps this is why Christ calls us to rest. He longs to provide what is lacking in our lives–something only He can provide.

In a Mediterranean culture where sleep may not have always been easy, Christ's call to rest held a powerful pull from the waves of life. In our world, we often likewise desire a slower pace, an extended pause. Whether then or now, His words continue to apply. If quiet is lacking in your heart, it may indicate a need for extended times not only of solitude, but time with the Savior. Only in Him will we experience true rest.

Share your experience now at
www.ThirstNoMoreBook.com.

"Take my yoke upon you and learn from me."
—Matthew 11:29

Our human desire longs for freedom. We seek liberation from any restraint that may restrict our ability to make free choices. Perhaps this is precisely why Jesus calls us to the opposite extreme—to take His yoke upon us—a seemingly harsh limitation upon our freedom.

A yoke was the restraint placed upon an ox for use in plowing a field. The ox had no option but to move ahead as its master requested. Likewise, Christ challenges us to take His yoke. Why? Not to treat us as livestock, but to direct us along the course He has prepared for us. Only under His guidance will we bear much fruit. Under His direction, we find true freedom, joy, and purpose for life.

Share your experience now at
www.ThirstNoMoreBook.com.

April 22

"Haven't you read?"
—Matthew 12:3

The Pharisees, an elite Jewish religious group, condemned Jesus and His followers for picking grain to eat on the Sabbath. This sacred day permitted no work. They had broken the Law of God.

When confronted, Jesus provided His own rebuke. He began with the convicting phrase, "Haven't you read?" Jesus provides multiple examples to show their actions were well within God's purposes. Before we judge the actions of others, we do well to examine our own souls as well as God's Word. At times, confrontation is needed; but sometimes what needs confronting is our own attitudes. We must continually seek God's truth by reading it. Then we can know it, live it, and share it with others. May Christ grant us this lifestyle.

Share your experience now at
www.ThirstNoMoreBook.com.

"The Son of Man is Lord of the Sabbath."
—Matthew 12:8

Some scholars have argued that Jesus never claimed to be Messiah. Yet in one phrase He provides three teachings unique only to God's Son. First, He calls Himself the Son of Man. This title connected Jesus to the prophet Daniel who spoke of the coming Son of Man generations before Christ's earthly birth in Bethlehem.

Second, the word "Lord" presented a reference to Himself as God, not simply a master or ancient equivalent of "Sir." We know this because of the third phrase, "of the Sabbath." Only the God of Israel had established the Sabbath as a sacred day. Only God could call Himself Lord of the Sabbath. Jesus made clear who He was. Have we made clear our devotion to Him?

Share your experience now at
www.ThirstNoMoreBook.com.

"How much more valuable."
—Matthew 12:12

A man with a shriveled hand sat among those in the synagogue with Jesus. There, the religious teachers tested Him by asking, "Is it lawful to heal on the Sabbath?" Jesus knew their hearts, and cut to the core of the issue. He answered, "How much more valuable is a person than a sheep?" The rhetorical answer? "Much more valuable."

God cares for all His creation, animals included. But God always places the highest priority on human life. In this case, Jesus used this conviction in the process of healing a crippled man. In a broader sense, we must see all human life as sacred. We are created in God's image; let us treat one another accordingly. We are of infinite value in God's sight.

Share your experience now at
www.ThirstNoMoreBook.com.

"He will proclaim justice to the nations."
—Matthew 12:18

Quoting the prophet Isaiah, Matthew notes Jesus would "proclaim justice to the nations." What is this justice? We often think of justice in the sense of vengeance. Some person or some thing is wrong and requires vindication. Yet Jesus provides justice in a much deeper sense. In Him, justice includes proclaiming truth, living truth, bringing truth.

We, likewise, share in both proclaiming truth and living it through our lives. "Bringing truth," however, belongs to Christ alone. When He returns, He will right all injustice. Until then, our calling is to share and live the truth of Christ, helping all those we can in the process. We proclaim justice now; He will provide ultimate justice in the future, a justice that is perfect and without end.

Share your experience now at
www.ThirstNoMoreBook.com.

"The kingdom of God has come upon you."
—Matthew 12:28

Jesus spoke frequently of the kingdom. Yet in His response to His critics about His power over demons, refers to Himself, saying, "The kingdom of God has come upon you." As leader of the kingdom of God, this makes sense. Yet this insight provides one further detail about our eternal resting place.

If Jesus refers to Himself when He discusses the kingdom, it is clear the kingdom is where He is. Our heavenly home will not only exist among saints of past and present, but in His very presence. This creates a longing and anticipation in our lives for the time when we who trust in Him will be with Him. If today causes us trouble, know a time to be in His perfect presence is near.

Share your experience now at
www.ThirstNoMoreBook.com.

"Whoever is not with me is against me."
—Matthew 12:30

We are either with Jesus or against Him. Jesus leaves no middle ground. Some areas of faith allow for ambiguity; commitment to Christ requires complete allegiance.

In speaking to His critics, Jesus removed any doubt regarding a half-hearted response to His message. He seeks those who seek Him fully; He desires people who desire Him completely. If we falter in our dedication along the way, we must return to our first love. He deserves nothing less. Just as Christ's message was undivided, so our lives must be undivided in response. He both desires and deserves our total dedication. Anything less stands opposed to His way. Our lives only find fulfillment as our way submits to His way with reckless abandon.

Share your experience now at
www.ThirstNoMoreBook.com.

"The mouth speaks what the heart is full of."
—Matthew 12:34

Our song reflects its source. The words we share gush as an overflow of the heart. Jesus knew this truth, mentioning it in response to His hard-hearted critics. Their hearts were hard; so were their words.

The implications of this statement pour through every facet of our lives. What we view, read, listen to, the people we spend the most time with, our music, the messages on our clothing or walls. Each communicates to ourselves and those around us either light or darkness. We must seek to fill ourselves with light. As we do, our words provide light to those around us. Choose what enters our hearts wisely and what comes out will be wisdom. Choose what enters with love; out will flow love.

Share your experience now at
www.ThirstNoMoreBook.com.

APRIL 29

"We want to see a sign."
—Matthew 12:38

Our Savior's skeptics sought a sign. A sign would "prove" Jesus was Messiah; a miracle would make His claims legitimate. But Jesus would have none of it. He labeled their request as "wicked." He had already healed, cast out demons, and spoken with authority. He was a walking fulfillment of prophecy. Yet they still sought a sign.

It is easy to point at these doubters and say, "Yeah, Jesus, tell them!" Yet we often find ourselves in the role of skeptic. We ask God for signs when we already know His decision; we seek confirmation when Christ has made clear His will in areas of our lives. In short, we doubt because we lack faith. Rather than a sign, let us seek our Savior.

Share your experience now at
www.ThirstNoMoreBook.com.

"Here are my mother and brothers."
—Matthew 12:49

Our world speaks of family very loosely. In the ancient world, family was sacred. Ancestral lines, generational traditions, and abiding rituals pervaded family life. When Mary and the siblings of Jesus arrived to meet Him, someone announced His family had arrived. Jesus used this event as an enduring, teachable moment.

Likely spreading His hands before His audience, He asked, "Who is my mother, and who are my brothers?" His answer? The one who does the will of the Father. In a few words, Jesus radically redefined family based on blood to a family based on His blood. Family was no longer focused on this world's definition, but a heavenly vision for those who followed Christ. Let us live as the family of God this day.

Share your experience now at
www.ThirstNoMoreBook.com.

MAY 1

"He told them many things in parables."
—Matthew 13:3

Parables are stories. Jesus frequently communicating through story the deep spiritual truths of the kingdom. Matthew's first parable, for example, focuses on four types of seed. Those listening would have innately known Jesus approved only of the fourth seed. Planted on the good soil, it flourished.

The story's goal presented a dilemma for Christ's listeners. Living an unresponsive or superficial life was unacceptable; the only appropriate response was to "produce a crop." We are to accept the message of Christ and multiply it. Anything less is not good seed; anything less misses the story. Later, Jesus would unpack its meaning to His disciples. Here, we are encouraged to see the field, the seed, and the crop. We are called to feel the story, then live it.

Share your experience now at
www.ThirstNoMoreBook.com.

MAY 2

"Whoever has will be given more."
—Matthew 13:12

Christ's words often puzzled His closest followers. When they asked why He spoke in parables, His answer included the equally enigmatic phrase, "Whoever has will be given more." Some suggest this refers to additional insight given the disciples. Others interpret the words as a parallel to the upcoming quote from Isaiah.

Either way, the core of this thought involves a group of people who receive abundance. In Christ, we are the ones who have been given everything needed for life and godliness. Yet He continues to bless us each day with more than we deserve. Rather than stand perplexed at His gifts, we can offer praise for His generosity. Let us live a life of thanksgiving to our Lord, the Source of every perfect gift.

Share your experience now at
www.ThirstNoMoreBook.com.

"I would heal them."
—Matthew 13:15

God has always offered healing. Jesus made such ability strikingly clear through raising the dead, removing leprosy, and restoring sight. But God's soothing power has existed from eternity past. In quoting Isaiah, Jesus highlights the overwhelming response of God to those who respond: "I would heal them."

These words still live for our time and our hearts. If we run to Him, He answers us. If we seek refuge in His arms, He holds us. If we stumble to Him with wounded heart, He will heal us. The only condition is our surrender. He calls us see with our eyes, hear with our ear, understand with our hearts and turn. Let us come to Him; let us accept the healing of the Great Physician.

Share your experience now at
www.ThirstNoMoreBook.com.

MAY 4

"I will utter things hidden."
—Matthew 13:35

Jesus spoke in parables not simply for impact; He did so to fulfill prophecy. Matthew refers to this, quoting Psalm 78, "I will utter things hidden." In an interesting twist, the poetry of the psalmist predicted the stories of the Savior.

To the crowds, the stories provided entertainment in addition to education. To the disciples, parables became a critical discussion point. On multiple occasions, the disciples referred to Christ's stories, seeking understanding. Jesus spoke to His attentive followers of these hidden things in a way that shaped their lives for further service. Likewise, Christ desires us to ask tough questions and learn the ways of God. When we ask, we resemble His closest followers. When He answers, we develop a deeper appreciation of His Word.

Share your experience now at
www.ThirstNoMoreBook.com.

"The righteous will shine like the sun."
—Matthew 13:43

The kingdom thrived as a dominant theme in Christ's parables. Jesus once explained to His disciples that His people will "shine like the sun" in the kingdom. Why? Everything that causes sin and all evil will be removed. All that will remain is Christ, His kingdom, and those who belong to Him.

In contrast, those who do not believe will suffer eternally. We may struggle temporarily, but will receive relief in eternity. Many do not share our future hope. Until we enter eternity with Christ, it is both our job and urgent desire to communicate His love to all who will listen. We do not share Jesus to offend or for mere obedience. We share Christ so others may shine like the sun.

Share your experience now at
www.ThirstNoMoreBook.com.

MAY 6

"They took offense at him."
—Matthew 13:57

Nazareth: the hometown of Jesus. Readers would expect a warm reception, perhaps even a parade. The local hero had returned from a speaking tour complete with awe-inspiring healings. News about Him had traveled across the nation.

But Matthew's Gospel informs us of a different reality. Rather than rejoice in Christ's abilities, His hometown took offense at Him. They questioned His education, His healing powers, even His family. We are told Jesus did few miracles there due to their skepticism. Familiarity often breeds apathy and insensitivity. May we who know Christ reject the temptation to treat our Lord flippantly. Rather, may we embrace Him each morning as our Teacher, Healer, and Savior. Let us not take offense; let us make our lives an offering.

Share your experience now at
www.ThirstNoMoreBook.com.

"This is John the Baptist! He has risen."
—Matthew 14:2

Herod believed Jesus was a resurrection of John, the man he had sentenced to death. The disciples would long remember this case of mistaken identity, though they rejected the error. Yet Herod has not been the only person to attribute the works of Christ to someone or something else. We routinely dismiss the hand of Christ in favor of even the most bizarre explanations to somehow rationalize situations.

Jesus works in our lives to honor to His name. When we attribute His interventions to other factors, we make ourselves in our own form of Herod. We must carefully observe God's work in our lives and acknowledge His supernatural abilities. As we do, the true message of Jesus spreads, drawing attention to Him.

Share your experience now at
www.ThirstNoMoreBook.com.

"You give them something to eat."
—Matthew 14:16

Jesus often used food to teach spiritual lessons. As the day drew near an end, His disciples urged Him to send the crowd away to prepare an evening meal. Instead, Jesus answered, "You give them something to eat." The disciples responded in human terms. "We don't have that kind of food. We only have five loaves of bread and a few fish."

But five plus two equaled enough for Jesus to feed thousands. What made the difference? Jesus did. He revealed once again His power over the natural realm. Still today, we often respond to His challenges with, "We don't have those kinds of resources. That's impossible!" But that is precisely what Jesus desires—to use His children to accomplish the impossible for His glory.

Share your experience now at
www.ThirstNoMoreBook.com.

"The disciples picked up twelve basketfuls."
—Matthew 14:20

Jesus clearly had a sense of humor. He had just used His disciples to feed thousands of people with only five loaves of bread and two fish. Now He had them collect the remaining food. The amount? Twelve basketfuls, 1 basketful for each disciple.

What was Jesus communicating? We are not told the entire story. But we can guess they did not soon forget the day they each carried a basket of leftover heavier than the entire original meal. Jesus vividly portrayed His ability to provide above and beyond our human needs. The picture He presented His disciples on that day remains both a humorous and impressive example for us today. Jesus can provide for our every need—no matter our humble means.

Share your experience now at
www.ThirstNoMoreBook.com.

*"He went up on a mountainside
by himself to pray."*
—Matthew 14:23

Prayer is essential to our spiritual lives. Just as we cannot live without breathing, our souls cannot endure without praying. After an intense day, Jesus paused for an extended time "by himself to pray." We are not told what He said or how long He remained. The emphasis in the words notes sustained, contemplative communication with God.

Afterwards Jesus would plunge again into the many endeavors of His Father. But at this moment, He concentrated on one endeavor—prayer. In our pursuit of God's work, we can easily miss God's worth. In our busy pursuits, we can neglect our singular purpose—the glory of God our Father. Let us go to the mountain alone, let us disappear from the noise of the crowd, and pray.

Share your experience now at
www.ThirstNoMoreBook.com.

"Take courage! It is I. Don't be afraid."
—Matthew 14:27

Humans fixate on fear. From pranks to films, entire industries are built both to create and prevent fear. Fear is part of our human makeup. The disciples feared when a storm endangered their boat, placing their lives at risk. There feared once again when Jesus appeared to them upon the water. At first, they believed He was a ghost.

Jesus addressed their fear: "Take courage! It is I. Do not fear." The last time they feared the storm, Jesus slept on the boat; this time He stood on the water. Fear existed in both cases; Jesus also challenged their fear both times. When Jesus is with us, we can endure any storm. When He is near, we can overcome any wave.

Share your experience now at
www.ThirstNoMoreBook.com.

MAY 12

"Why did you doubt?"
—Matthew 14:31

Jesus questions our doubt. Peter experienced this principle in a dramatic manner. In his boldness, He said if it was really Jesus walking on water, then let him join Christ on the water. Called by Jesus, Peter stepped over the edge of the boat.

We are initially impressed with Peter's bravery. But along the way, he takes His eyes away from Jesus and drops into the sea. He cries out for help, Jesus grabs his hand, and they climb into the boat. Rather than a ribbon, Jesus offers a rebuke. Faith is not designed for only a few steps; faith grows when exercised, whether walking on water or in our own spiritual journeys. Let us walk in faith, eyes fixed on Jesus.

Share your experience now at
www.ThirstNoMoreBook.com.

"Truly you are the Son of God."
—Matthew 14:33

The first time Matthew mentioned the title "Son of God" was when Satan questioned Christ's resolve in the wilderness. After Jesus walks on water, His disciples first make the vocal pronouncement, "Truly you are the Son of God." They moved beyond doubt and discussion to a point of decision.

Each believer draws this same conclusion at some point in his or her faith journey. At first, we all question Christ, wondering if He is truly relevant. Later, we decide to discuss our thoughts about Christ, interacting with the views of others on matters of belief. Finally comes the necessary decision point when we declare Jesus is the Son of God. Do you remember this time in your life? He is truly the Son of God.

Share your experience now at
www.ThirstNoMoreBook.com.

*"And why do you break the command
of God for...your tradition?"*
—Matthew 15:3

Faith includes traditions. Sometimes these traditions stand in the way of the faith. The Jewish tradition of Jesus' time was to ceremonially wash hands before meals. This was not an issue of hygiene; it was considered a matter of godliness. The fact that the disciples did not participate made them disrespected by others.

Jesus answered their confrontation with confrontation of His own: "Why do you break the command of God for the sake of your tradition?" He taught it was not about what we put into our bodies that make us unclean but what comes out of our mouths. Jesus has always given priority to the soul over our ceremonies. What will we speak today? Let us strive to share words clean and holy to Him.

Share your experience now at
www.ThirstNoMoreBook.com.

"Woman, you have great faith!"
—Matthew 15:28

We often believe Jesus said yes to every request for healing. However, when an immigrant woman pleaded for mercy for her possessed daughter, He initially declined. Why? His mission was to Israel, not her people. But she remained resilient. Rather than turn away discouraged, she pleaded again, noting even dogs eat the crumbs that fall from their master's table.

Jesus noted her act as a bold step of faith. While religious leaders questioned and mocked His abilities, this woman reasoned with Him on behalf of her daughter. In response, He answered, "Woman, you have great faith! Your request is granted." Perhaps God sometimes delays His reply to our requests not to discourage us, but to embolden our faith. Let us pray with unrelenting faith.

Share your experience now at
www.ThirstNoMoreBook.com.

"How many loaves do you have?"
—Matthew 15:34

Jesus had given the past three days to teaching and healing thousands of men, women, and children who had come to the wilderness to see Him. As evening approached, He had compassion on these people, mentioning His desire to feed them. His disciples asked the obvious, "Where could we get enough bread?"

In response, Jesus responded, "How many loaves do you have?" The disciples perhaps began to realize His plan at this moment. The Messiah who had fed over 5,000 and healed disease wanted to feed a crowd. Limitations would not stop Him. The people would eat and be satisfied. We often bring Christ our doubts, yet He already has a plan prepared. We must only stay close to Him each step of the way.

Share your experience now at
www.ThirstNoMoreBook.com.

"Jesus left them and went away."
—Matthew 16:4

Religious leaders continued to demand miracles from Jesus. Just as when tempted by Satan in the wilderness, Jesus resisted the push to use His powers for popularity. Instead, He claimed only the wicked seek a sign. He pointed them to the example of Jonah, a man called by God who at first refused to obey His will.

Jesus invested days with His disciples; He had little time for religious legalists. His desire for us is not to develop into Pharisees, but to develop intimacy. Such intimacy reflects the character of Christ, His maturity, His love. Only then will we walk worthy of our calling; only then can we truly live as one worthy of the title Christian, one who lives like Christ.

Share your experience now at
www.ThirstNoMoreBook.com.

"Do you still not understand?"
—Matthew 16:9

The disciples frequently struggled to make sense of their Leader's teachings. When He warned about the bread of the Pharisees and Sadducees, they initially thought it was because they had forgotten to pack bread for their trip.

We often take Christ's words and attempt to apply them to areas they do not belong. Why? Often, our hearts are focused on the here and now, our bread, our needs. But Jesus keeps pointing toward spiritual realities. He seeks to train us in holiness. When confused by something we believe is of Christ, we would do well to ask, "What will bring Him glory?" When we do, we will help avoid the teachings of the Pharisees and Sadducees; we'll find joy at the voice of our Savior.

Share your experience now at
www.ThirstNoMoreBook.com.

MAY 19

"Who do you say I am?"
—Matthew 16:15

People hold many views about Jesus. Some believe He was a myth, others simply a man. Scholars debate His ethics; mystics highlight His love. The same took place when He walked the earth. Jesus used this controversy to clarify the view of His own followers by first asking, "Who do people say the Son of Man is?"

John the Baptist, Elijah, Jeremiah, and other prophets had each been mentioned. But then Jesus made the issue personal: "Who do you say I am?" Peter correctly answered, "You are the Messiah, the Son of the living God." Only when we can answer as Peter did have we grasped the true view of Christ. He was not a myth or merely man; He was and is Messiah.

Share your experience now at
www.ThirstNoMoreBook.com.

*"Whoever wants to be my disciple
must deny themselves."*
—Matthew 16:24

To follow Christ requires us to quit following self. In the words of Jesus, we must first deny self. Second, we must take up our cross. This cross represented suffering and death. Third, we must follow Christ. All three are necessary to true discipleship.

If we do not deny self, we promote self. If we do not take up our cross, we walk apart from the cross. If we do not follow Christ, we follow someone or something else. True spiritual development is often a painful process, because we can no longer live as we desire but rather as He desires. Believing in Jesus is free; becoming like Jesus is costly. Let us count the cost, take up our cross, and follow Christ.

Share your experience now at
www.ThirstNoMoreBook.com.

"What good will it be?"
—Matthew 16:26

The soul is priceless. How can we know? Jesus taught, "What good will it be for someone to gain the whole world, yet forfeit their soul?" One soul's value exceeds the riches of all the earth. In comparison to the entire world's price tag, the soul is priceless.

The value of life cannot be determined by a price tag. Whatever the cost, regardless of the commitment required, we must develop a soul that seeks God. Beyond our own soul, we must consider the souls of others. No worldly pursuit compares to the joy of experiencing the change of one soul from death to life. The call of Jesus is clear—pursue a life of heavenly rewards; not a life of earthly riches.

Share your experience now at
www.ThirstNoMoreBook.com.

"This is my Son, whom I love."
—Matthew 17:5

Peter, James, and John joined Jesus for a unique time in which Moses and Elijah appeared on a mountaintop with Jesus. Their Teacher stood transfigured before them, His clothes sparkling white. A bright cloud covered them as well, with the very voice of God speaking.

These three men heard the Father speak to the Son: "This is my Son, whom I love; with him I am well pleased. Listen to him!" These are the greatest words a father can communicate to a child. Jesus would express this same love when He gave His life on our behalf. As the Father spoke to His Son, He speaks to us today, "You are my child; with you I am well pleased." We are loved by our Father.

Share your experience now at
www.ThirstNoMoreBook.com.

"Nothing will be impossible for you."
—Matthew 17:20

Jesus had given His disciples authority over demons. But in one case, His followers could not overpower a particular demon. The son's mother knelt before Jesus and begged for mercy for her son. After Jesus did show mercy, His disciples asked about their inability to heal the boy.

His answer? "Because you have so little faith." In at least some cases, the reason our requests remain unanswered is due to our lack of faith. But with faith, Jesus taught nothing would be impossible. Even faith the size of a mustard seed can move mountains. Rather than be discouraged, we are challenged to develop deeper faith. Why? Lack of faith is our only limitation. With faith, God can use us to do even the impossible.

Share your experience now at
www.ThirstNoMoreBook.com.

*"Who, then, is the greatest
in the kingdom of heaven?"*
—Matthew 18:1

A close study of the disciples reveals they were often concerned about status. Some requested to sit at Christ's right and left in the kingdom; others wished to stop His death by use of force. On another occasion, they asked, "Who, then, is the greatest in the kingdom of heaven?"

His answer stood upside down in His culture. Pointing toward a child, He challenged His followers to take the lowly position of a child to be greatest in the kingdom. The least will be the greatest. The kingdom includes difficult teachings, perhaps none more perplexing than the fact we lead best through serving. The greatest in the kingdom will be those with pure, childlike faith. This is what our Father desires.

Share your experience now at
www.ThirstNoMoreBook.com.

"Do not despise one of these little ones."
—Matthew 18:10

God notes a special favor toward children. He specifically taught that we must not despise or look down on one of these "little ones." God provides angels from His own presence who watch over them. He expects a similar response from us.

Why children? Weak and vulnerable, children are often mistreated in ways that scar for a lifetime. Yet children also represent the innocent, simple faith He desires of us. Perhaps the best way to satisfy both teachings is to live out our faith among children. As we do, we show His love and better understand the love He desires from us. God watches over His children with angels. He expects us to care for children with a similar compassion. Our children must be our priority.

Share your experience now at
www.ThirstNoMoreBook.com.

May 26

"Just between the two of you."
—Matthew 18:15

Conflict crushes relationships. Jesus knew this, providing clear direction for these difficult situations. The first necessary step is to take the issue directly to the other person. This alone would solve a vast number of conflicts we encounter in our daily interactions.

Yet how often we miss this! It is much easier to rant to someone else, nurture our hurt to ourselves, or go public with our complaints. But these alternatives lead to unhealthy ends. Despite the difficulty presented in direct discussion, the outcome is typically much more positive than other routes. Refuse to avoid friends who offend. Reconcile. Restore. Return the relationship to health through the challenge of taking personal conflict "just between the two of you." When they listen, "you have won them over."

Share your experience now at
www.ThirstNoMoreBook.com.

"How many times shall I forgive?"
—Matthew 18:21

Forgiveness is difficult. Peter once asked Jesus, "How many times shall I forgive?" The Jewish tradition was 7. Jesus responded with 70 times 7.* The point was not the number of times, but an endless number of times. Just as Jesus does not keep track of wrongs forgiven, He expects His children to stop counting how many times we forgive others.

The focus is not on how little we can forgive, but how much we can forgive. Our human inclination is to keep score; God's will is for us to lose track of the score. As we have been forgiven we are to forgive. We could never "out forgive" Christ; we are instead to "always forgive" those who offend us. "How many times?" Every time.

* Some translations say "seventy-seven times."

Share your experience now at
www.ThirstNoMoreBook.com.

"It was not this way from the beginning."
—Matthew 19:8

Separation hurts. Whether dealing with a broken marriage, friendship, or other relationship, there is deep human pain. Jesus was aware of this. When challenged on the issue of divorce, His response speaks deeply to the hurt of our time: "It was not this way from the beginning."

God did not create human relationships for disunity, but community. When we destroy a relationship, marriage or otherwise, we experience the pain of living in ways God did not develop as part of His original design. While we may suffer the sting of broken relationships in this life, we can look forward to a day where relationships will be made perfect once again. There, in the presence of Christ, we can enjoy relationship as God intended.

Share your experience now at
www.ThirstNoMoreBook.com.

"What good thing must I do?"
—Matthew 19:16

A successful young man once came to Jesus to ask, "What good thing must I do to get eternal life?" Jesus knew his heart and suggested a response specific to his attachment to worldly possessions. Rather than start with the message of eternal life in Christ, Jesus challenged the man's idols.

"Sell your possessions and give to the poor.... Then come, follow me." This single condition crushed the confidence of this man. Give up his status? Give up my life to follow Jesus? It was too much. Many have suggested we can live for Christ and continue to embrace the things of this world. Jesus made clear this was not an option. We are called to make Him priority over all else, regardless of cost.

Share your experience now at
www.ThirstNoMoreBook.com.

"Many who are last will be first."
—Matthew 19:30

We must give up to go up. In the kingdom, many who are last will be first. This equation makes little sense in this world, but is the way of Christ for those who wonder, as Peter, "What then will there be for us?" To follow Christ requires a downward career track that does not depend on dollars or status. Instead, what matters is Christ.

Daily, we fight temptations to embrace the world's competitive nature. We are told to "Get ahead," "Don't let others take advantage of you," "Stand up for your rights." But Jesus often calls us to get behind, give up our advantages, and give up our rights. When we do, we move downward on this world's charts, but upward in the kingdom.

Share your experience now at
www.ThirstNoMoreBook.com.

"Are you envious because I am generous?"
—Matthew 20:15

Envy is part of our flawed human nature. We seek to stand above the next person, to receive honor, to receive acclaim. This is even true with God's grace. When someone with a sordid past embraces Jesus, we can be tempted to say, "What about me? I've served longer. I've remained faithful through years of difficulty."

God knows this; but He is also generous. His grace reaches some as a child; others on their dying day. What matters is that we accept His grace. When we do, we become family with all those who know Christ until the day when we dwell with Him together for eternity. When others receive His grace, it is because He is generous; this should be our response as well.

Share your experience now at
www.ThirstNoMoreBook.com.

JUNE 1

"Whoever wants to become great…
must be your servant."
—Matthew 20:26

The answer to success in the kingdom is service. When two disciples sought priority in the kingdom, Jesus reminded them of this. Those who wish to stand tallest must kneel lowest.

Jesus not only taught servanthood, He modeled it. He came not to be served, but to serve, to give His life as a ransom for many. If we are uncertain how to begin, we begin with reflecting His life— King of kings, yet Servant of all; Creator of life, yet giving His life. Becoming a servant does not consist of a title or rights; becoming a servant involves a resignation of rights. To become great, we must become godly. To be first, we must become last. Only then will we be great in God's eyes.

Share your experience now at
www.ThirstNoMoreBook.com.

June 2

"What do you want me to do for you?"
—Matthew 20:32

When we cry out to God, He does not sit back uninterested. Instead, He listens attentively. He even seeks how He can help. In the case of two blind men who called for mercy from Jesus, He stepped from His busy travels to ask for their request. Their answer? "We want our sight."

Jesus had compassion on them and gave them their sight. His response reveals His attitude toward our petitions. We cry out, He asks for our plea, and we offer our heart's desire. When He sees the desire of our heart, compassion wells up from His infinite love. He answers as only He can. May we, as the men who received their sight, respond by faithfully following Him, the Son of David.

Share your experience now at
www.ThirstNoMoreBook.com.

JUNE 3

"Who is this?"
—Matthew 21:10

When we celebrate our King, people notice. When they notice, they ask questions. When people ask questions, we have an opportunity to share Jesus. Such conversations clearly took place the day Jesus rode into Jerusalem on a donkey to the acclaim of many. The whole city was "stirred." The people asked, "Who is this?"

The crowd responded, "Jesus, the prophet from Nazareth in Galilee." They clearly identified His name and His role. As we live in worship of Christ, the overflow is to communicate who Jesus is to those curious friends we encounter throughout our journey. When we confidently speak of Jesus, others often desire to know more about Christ. Let us worship and prepare to share this reason for the hope within us.

Share your experience now at
www.ThirstNoMoreBook.com.

"My house will be called a house of prayer."
—Matthew 21:13

When worshippers traveled to the temple at Passover, animal sacrifices were made. Rather than bringing doves or other livestock with them, adherents would bring money to make purchases in the temple courts. Some had to exchange funds; others simply purchased doves. But what had originated as a true need had become a profit-making venture. This profiting from religion infuriated Jesus.

In this instance, Jesus overturned tables and benches to make His point: "My house will be called a house of prayer." The temple was for God, not financial gain. God's grace must not be tainted by greed; our message must not be motivated by money. Through devotion to prayer, we can resist our human inclination for greed and simply worship Him.

Share your experience now at
www.ThirstNoMoreBook.com.

"If you believe."
—Matthew 21:22

What do a fig tree and faith have in common? Much, according to Jesus. He spoke against a fruitless fig tree. It withered instantly. Amazed, His disciples ask how it had happened. Jesus used their curiosity to address the issue of faith.

Jesus noted belief involves both faith and a lack of doubt. With such belief, we can move mountains. We can receive whatever we ask in prayer. Then why do many prayers remain unanswered? Sometimes God has other plans in store. Yet our faith plays a role at times. If we believe when we pray, we can be confident God's replies are exactly what we need, without doubting His will. His determines the answer. Our part is to prayer in faith: "If you believe."

Share your experience now at
www.ThirstNoMoreBook.com.

"He is not the God of the dead but of the living."
—Matthew 22:32

The religious group known as the Sadducees taught there was no resurrection. Jesus spoke against their faulty belief, noting, "He is not the God of the dead but of the living." Quoting Exodus, He noted God's promise as the God of Abraham, Isaac, and Jacob. His emphasis is that those patriarchs were considered alive after their earthly departure even in the Law of Moses.

Jesus condemned this group for not knowing "the Scriptures or the power of God." The Scriptures taught that those who believe live forever. The power of God makes this possible. We do not know every detail about the afterlife, but we do know this—God's children live forever with Him. God's power makes this belief reality, one that comforts us today.

Share your experience now at
www.ThirstNoMoreBook.com.

"Teacher, which is the greatest commandment?"
—Matthew 22:36

A religious expert presented a question to reveal Christ's perspective on God's Law: "Teacher, which is the greatest commandment?" Jesus was clear in answering to love God fully and to love your neighbor as yourself.

No further reply is mentioned here. Why? Jesus had answered the Law with the Law. Both of His response quoted words from Scripture. When others challenge our faith, we need only respond that our goal is to love God and love people. We may not agree in every matter of faith, but we must all agree this is the greatest commandment. Yet it is not enough to know it; our ultimate goal must be to live it, like Jesus. We must continually remember our goal—to love God, and to love our neighbor.

Share your experience now at
www.ThirstNoMoreBook.com.

"Those who humble themselves will be exalted."
—Matthew 23:12

Humility was Christ's answer to many issues of His time. The religious and political leaders of His nation enjoyed the power of title and influence. Jesus warned against such pride. Instead of calling one another "Rabbi" or "Father," He reminded His followers they were family. Rather than rulers, they were to live as fellow servants.

Do we find similar influences tainting our walk with God? Have career or reputation taken the place of living as servant or family? If so, the answer is humility. God promises to humble those who exalt themselves; to exalt those who humble themselves. We cannot both promote Savior and self. We must serve Christ and humble ourselves before the Lord. He will lift us up.

Share your experience now at
www.ThirstNoMoreBook.com.

JUNE 9

"My words will never pass away."
—Matthew 24:35

God's words last forever. Though the skies and earth will one day end, what Christ speaks will endure. How is this possible? First, we know God is eternal. His words, an extension of Himself, will last forever as well. Second, Christ has conquered death. If He cannot be destroyed, neither can His words. What He says is true and lasting.

When a friend shares words of hope, we can trust they are likely true. But friends sometimes let us down. God, however, is more than a friend. His words are always true. What He says has come to pass in the past; what He predicts will come to pass in the future. We need not doubt His word, but discover it, living it out today.

Share your experience now at
www.ThirstNoMoreBook.com.

JUNE 10

"Therefore keep watch."
—Matthew 24:42

Jesus spoke frequently about the future. In doing so, He often stressed we are to "keep watch." Why? Because His timing is not our timing. Jesus promises to return at a moment we do not expect, along a timeline we cannot predict.

Our human nature typically presses us in one of two directions. Some of us are more inclined to believe Jesus will never return, living without the urgency He expects. Others of us live with hyper-awareness, in danger of interpreting every life event as the last "sign" before His coming. Neither approach is healthy. What God desires is devoted service connected with an attitude that anticipates His coming. Only then will we "keep watch" as He challenged His hearers long ago.

Share your experience now at
www.ThirstNoMoreBook.com.

"Well done, good and faithful servant!"
—Matthew 25:21

God has granted each of us special abilities. Whether called spiritual gifts, sacred talents, or another label, we recognize our Father provides unique capabilities designed specifically for our role in this world. In Christ's parable of the talents, each servant is given certain amounts. Each servant, but one, used their gift faithfully. Each servant, but one, heard, "Well done, good and faithful servant!"

When we stand before our heavenly Father, we will not concern ourselves with our cars, our homes, or our bank accounts. Instead, all that will matter is, "Well done, good and faithful servant." We must live faithfully now to us to hear those words then. We must not settle for the applause of men; we must seek the joy of the Master.

Share your experience now at
www.ThirstNoMoreBook.com.

JUNE 12

"I was hungry and you gave me something to eat."
—Matthew 25:35

What we do for others, we do to Christ. What we do not do for others, we do not do to Christ. The most striking example of this concept is found in Christ's story of the sheep and the goats. His sheep were those who fed the hungry, clothed the naked, cared for the sick, visited those in prison. The goats were those who did not.

Why does Jesus make these actions a defining line for service in the kingdom? In His words, "Whatever you did for one of the least of these...you did for me." Serving the least of these is serving Christ. Let us serve Christ through serving those He loves. Let us feed the hungry; let us offer water to the thirsty.

Share your experience now at
www.ThirstNoMoreBook.com.

"She has done a beautiful thing to me."
—Matthew 26:10

As Jesus shared a meal with His disciples, an unnamed woman appeared with an expensive jar of alabaster oil. In love, she poured it on His head. Those with Him complained, suggesting the money could have been better spent on the poor. But Jesus defended the woman's action. "Why are you bothering this woman? She has done a beautiful thing to me."

It is easier to discredit the offering of another than to bring our own extravagant gift to Jesus. Her act would not only prepare for Christ's burial, as He mentions, but would be written down in Scripture as an example of full devotion. We need not seek the approval of others; we need only to bring our greatest possible gift before our Lord.

Share your experience now at
www.ThirstNoMoreBook.com.

"Take and eat; this is my body."
—Matthew 26:26

When the disciples shared a Passover meal with Jesus, they had no idea it would be their last. For His followers, the event was gratifying. For Jesus, the event was good-bye. To commemorate this final meal, Jesus gave thanks and handed out unleavened bread, speaking the famous words, "Take and eat; this is my body."

Jesus sat in their midst; how could He claim this bread was His body? Scholars still debate this statement. Perhaps the best understanding is one of remembrance. Their Messiah desired to leave a physical act for His followers to recall their time together. He loved His friends; now He would leave them. Yet He would not leave them without a symbol of His love. Remember His love for us today.

Share your experience now at
www.ThirstNoMoreBook.com.

JUNE 15

"This is my blood of the covenant."
—Matthew 26:28

Blood is the symbol of life. In naming the wine at the Last Supper "my blood," Jesus intended for us to reflect upon His life poured out for our forgiveness. As red covered His body on the Cross, His followers would have a clear physical symbol to remind of His suffering.

We often seek to avoid reflection upon the suffering Christ endured. The agony overwhelms our emotions; the graphic nature of His death sickens our sensibilities. Yet Jesus desires for us to remember His pain. In doing so, we experience a deep appreciation for His sacrifice on our behalf; a renewed vigor to live our new lives. Let us remember His blood, poured out for us. Let us live in the forgiveness He has provided.

Share your experience now at
www.ThirstNoMoreBook.com.

"Not as I will, but as you will."
—Matthew 26:39

In the Lord's Prayer, Jesus taught us to pray, "Your will be done." In the prayer of our Lord, He prays, "Your will be done." Jesus teaches how to pray and shows how to pray. In the garden, His soul is overwhelmed at the pain He will soon endure. His human desire is to escape, but He does not. Instead, He prays, "Not as I will, but as you will."

His most faithful followers would soon fail Him. Peter would deny Him. The crowds He had taught would mock Him. Jesus knew all these things, yet still submitted Himself to God's will. May we, too, follow our Lord no matter the struggle; may we choose to say, "Not as I will, but as you will."

Share your experience now at
www.ThirstNoMoreBook.com.

"The spirit is willing, but the flesh is weak."
—Matthew 26:41

While Jesus prayed, His disciples slept. Upon His return, He woke them, instructing His men to join Him in prayer. Why? "The spirit is willing, but the flesh is weak." Our hearts often desire to cry out to God; our bodies often fail to comply. How do we resist this temptation? Watch and pray.

To watch and pray is different from simply praying. To watch and pray includes planning and preparation. If our prayertimes are weak, it may be due to lack of preparation. Do we have a time and place? Do we pray with others? Is there something specific to focus upon in prayer? When we give attention to prayer, prayer gets attention: "The spirit is willing, but the flesh is weak."

Share your experience now at
www.ThirstNoMoreBook.com.

"All who draw the sword will die by the sword."
—Matthew 26:52

Violence breeds violence. When Peter drew his sword and cut off the ear of an opponent, Jesus rebuked him. Why? Because He knew such an act would lead to Peter's death; this arrest had instead been prepared for the death of Jesus.

Yet the idea of "all who draw the sword will die by the sword" speaks still to our lives. When we choose violence, it leads others to choose violence. In the end, those who choose to live violently tend to die violently. But there is another way. Jesus modeled it. His way is to live the will of the Father. Our Father calls us to pray for our enemies and persecutors. Only then will we reflect the love of our Lord.

Share your experience now at
www.ThirstNoMoreBook.com.

"What shall I do, then, with Jesus?"
—Matthew 27:22

Pilate was caught in a dilemma. The religious leaders had presented a man they wished to put to death for blasphemy, yet Pilate found Jesus guilty of no crime. Rather than stand for Christ, Pilate turned to the crowd, asking, "What shall I do, then, with Jesus?"

Their answer? "Crucify him!" Despite offering Barabbas as a substitute and even washing his hands in innocence of Christ's death, Pilate turned Jesus over to His death. Pilate's actions, however, spoke louder than his words. He held the power of life and death and chose death. We, likewise, are given the opportunity to choose what we will do with Jesus. Will we stand for Christ or look to the crowd? What will we do with Jesus?

Share your experience now at
www.ThirstNoMoreBook.com.

"Surely he was the Son of God!"
—Matthew 27:54

When Jesus died, the earth reflected the Father's grief. The curtain of the temple was torn from top to bottom. A great earthquake occurred. Even the bodies of some who had died returned to life. This monumental combination of events caused those guarding Jesus at the Cross to exclaim, "Surely he was the Son of God!"

One of the clearest marks Jesus is God's Son is His impact on our world. His death rocked the planet; His resurrection has transformed the people of the nations. The Cross did not end His life; it offered the way to life. Two thousand years later, millions call to His name as Lord. Why? Not because of His fame or fortune, but because Jesus "was the Son of God!"

Share your experience now at
www.ThirstNoMoreBook.com.

"He has risen, just as he said."
—Matthew 28:6

Death could not conquer Jesus. The tomb could not hold Him. On the third day following His crucifixion, Jesus was alive! He had risen. He could give no greater example of His power than to defeat death and the grave. His followers would no longer grieve—they would rejoice.

When we experience the risen Jesus, two things take place. First, as with the women at the tomb, there is fear or awe. But both the angel and Jesus encouraged them not to fear. Instead, they were encouraged to tell His disciples. Second, there is joy. Only in the resurrected Jesus do we find true joy. Why? Because we have met the answer to death and eternal life—Jesus, the risen Christ.

Share your experience now at
www.ThirstNoMoreBook.com.

"All authority . . . has been given to me."
—Matthew 28:18

In defeating death, Jesus proved He held the ultimate power. Before ascending to heaven, He reminded His followers of this fact: "All authority on heaven and earth has been given to me." Why was this important? His final charge to them would only be possible with the power of God on their side.

Jesus would call His followers to make followers for Him from all nations, every group of people. They were to go, to baptize, to teach. A mission this great could only be accomplished with the authority of the risen Christ. This challenge to reach people for His name continues, whether next door or the next nation. The One with all authority has called us to communicate His message still today.

Share your experience now at
www.ThirstNoMoreBook.com.

"I am with you always."
—Matthew 28:20

The greatest comfort a friend can give is to be with us. Jesus promised this comfort in His final words before leaving earth, revealing, "I am with you always." His followers would face lonely days, intense struggle, even death. Christ's promise to be with them would come to mind during times of persecution and even in their final moments before martyrdom.

In our lives, this promise both reminds and anticipates. It reminds us of Christ's work on the Cross. It anticipates a coming day when we will be with Him in eternity. Until then, we are called to reflect His life in our own, sharing His love with all who will listen. Despite troubles in this life, we rest assured: "I am with you always."

Share your experience now at
www.ThirstNoMoreBook.com.

"Jesus got up, left the house and went off to a solitary place, where he prayed."
—Mark 1:35

The first step to intimacy with God is movement. For Jesus to pray, He first had to "get up." He also "left the house." Your bed may be a fine place to talk with God, but wakeful, disciplined intimacy frequently requires a change of location. Jesus modeled this concept of retreating to a solitary place alone with His heavenly Father.

We often focus only on the detail that Jesus prayed alone with the Father. What are overlooked are the preparations to be alone with God in a time and place where He would be uninterrupted. It is easy to pray when there are no interruptions; the difficult part is to prepare for it. Plan for time alone with God. You'll be much more likely to find it.

Share your experience now at
www.ThirstNoMoreBook.com.

"That they might be with him."
—Mark 3:14

We quickly realize Jesus chose 12 followers to help spread His message to others. However, He also had another reason—"that they might be with him." Unlike the crowds, who appeared for healing, teaching, or miracles, these disciples would work and live with Him during the quiet moments of the day.

An often-neglected insight in our relationship with Christ is that Christ calls us to both be with Him and serve Him. Both are essential, but it is this "being" we most frequently bypass. When we serve merely in our own strength, we miss the joys of His presence, a presence designed to refresh and prepare us for our times of service. Do not only live for Christ; live with Christ.

Share your experience now at
www.ThirstNoMoreBook.com.

"Come with me by yourselves."
—Mark 6:31

Rest matters. After His disciples returned from their travels, Jesus called them to, "Come with me by yourselves to a quiet place and get some rest." Rest includes both a physical and spiritual purpose. Our bodies must replenish strength through sleep and healing. Likewise, our souls must refuel through reflective time with our Lord.

Yet we frequently view rest as evil. Instead of a positive aspect of our journey, we eye relaxation as a negative necessity at best. Any sign of relaxation can be interpreted as laziness, not replenishment. Christ contradicts this way of human thinking. Our rest is as important as our work. But He has in mind more than sleep; Jesus desires unhurried time with us to meet us in the quiet place.

Share your experience now at
www.ThirstNoMoreBook.com.

JUNE 27

"Come with me by yourselves to a quiet place."
—Mark 6:31

Life devoted to Christ can be busy. The disciples quickly discovered this. They had just completed their first missionary work. The result? Exhaustion. Christ's response? Rest.

A common misunderstanding among Christ's followers is that we are to work constantly now and rest in eternity with God. But this is not the example of our Master. He has called us to serve and to savor. Without necessary times of reflection our work will soon grow weak in its impact.

Sometimes the greatest difference we can make is to rest. But respite alone is not enough. Our stillness must be with Him—"Come with me"—in order to follow His guidance and return to God's other purposes for our life with full vigor.

Share your experience now at
www.ThirstNoMoreBook.com.

JUNE 28

"Rest a little while."
—Mark 6:31

Rest is essential to serving God. Rather than a weakness, rest restores power physically and provides insight spiritually. Jesus often prayed alone and called His followers to spend time far from the eyes of the crowd.

Our humanness tempts us with thoughts that the world will not make it unless we work every waking moment. Even our dreams can betray us with an unhealthy focus on tasks yet incomplete. Yet God is in control. He desires time with you just as He asks for commitment from you. If you find yourself weak and weary at this moment, it may be your time to pull back, close your eyes, and as a simple child leaning against a father's shoulder, rest. Rest. Rest.

Share your experience now at
www.ThirstNoMoreBook.com.

"He has done everything well."
—Mark 7:37

Jesus healed on an unprecedented scale. The crowds were said to be "overwhelmed with amazement." Their response was, "He has done all things well." Yet crowds would later be involved in efforts to crucify Jesus. Could those who had experienced His healing power turn against Him?

This question can often be asked of our own lives. We have experienced the healing power of Christ, yet we often turn against Him in our time of need. Leaning on our own strength, we forget the Almighty God lives within us. He has healed us. He longs to help us again. Rather than turn against Him, let us keep our eyes fixed on Him, our Healer and Provider. "He has done everything well."

Share your experience now at
www.ThirstNoMoreBook.com.

"Do you see anything?"
—Mark 8:23

A blind man was once brought to Jesus for healing. He walked the blind man outside of the village and placed spit on his eyes, asking, "Do you see anything?" To the surprise of those watching, only a partial healing had taken place. He had regained vision, but a distorted reality.

Jesus then fully restored his sight. Why this two-part healing? Many suggest the act was to reveal the lack of understanding among His followers in the previous account. Despite many miracles, His disciples lacked faith. Yet following this blind man's healing, Peter boldly declared Jesus as Messiah. Something deep happened here. His followers realized they were the ones with a distorted reality. Only when they recognized Jesus as Messiah did they walk with clear vision.

Share your experience now at
www.ThirstNoMoreBook.com.

July 1

"Help me overcome my unbelief!"
—Mark 9:24

The father of a demon-possessed man presented his child to the disciples for healing. Their efforts failed. When Jesus arrived, the father asked for help "If you can." Jesus answered, "Everything is possible for the one who believes."

The father's answer offers abundant perspective: "I do believe; help me overcome my unbelief!" Can we both believe and still require help to conquer unbelief? This account points to yes. We may have faith in Christ, yet we find ourselves often walking in doubt. The answer is to believe and pray for increased faith. We ask for help to change and live like the change we pray to receive. He provided healing then; He will provide our healing now: "Help me overcome my unbelief!"

Share your experience now at
www.ThirstNoMoreBook.com.

"She...put in everything—all she had to live on."
—Mark 12:44

Giving reveals our heart. When Jesus and His followers watched those offering money at the temple, they spotted the large gifts of the wealthy mixed with the smaller gifts of those with less. But what Jesus highlighted was the woman who gave the least—only two small coins. She had not only offered a small gift in her poverty, she had given everything. "All she had to live on."

Financial giving discussions often take the form of which amount is best; what level is most appropriate. But Jesus shatters these conversations. He applauds the one who gives everything. He does not simply desire a tithe or special bonus; He desires our full allegiance. The amount is not what impresses Christ; the attitude is what He seeks.

Share your experience now at
www.ThirstNoMoreBook.com.

"The Lord has done this for me."
—Luke 1:25

How many times had she prayed for a son? We are not told, but Elizabeth had undoubtedly prayed multiple decades for a child to bring joy and continue the family name. In her later years, God had miraculously allowed her to become pregnant. In response, she declared, "The Lord has done this for me."

Too often we fail to acknowledge our blessings as gifts from God. Everything we have, from daily food to future plans, come from Him. Our attitude toward these gifts reveals the depth of our communion with God. When we are known for giving glory to His name, we become known as those who walk closely with Christ. Let us use this day to say, "The Lord has done this."

Share your experience now at
www.ThirstNoMoreBook.com.

JULY 4

"I am the Lord's servant."
—Luke 1:38

When the angel Gabriel appeared to Zechariah, he doubted. When Gabriel appeared to Mary, she submitted. In her words, "I am the Lord's servant." This single response highlights the life of a woman devoted to God, one who would become mother of Jesus. The rest of her life and the history of the world would be forever different from this one reply to God's message.

God sometimes calls us to an overwhelming journey. We can answer in doubt or in faith. The response of faith is one of a servant. When we choose to give up our rights to follow His way, He blesses us with opportunities unimaginable. When God speaks to us, let us respond as Mary, "I am the Lord's servant."

Share your experience now at
www.ThirstNoMoreBook.com.

JULY 5

"My soul magnifies the Lord."
—Luke 1:46 (ESV)

After meeting with her relative Elizabeth, Mary broke into song. The combination of the angel's visit to both women and Elizabeth's blessing upon Mary spurred her spirit to express words of praise to the Father. Her opening phrase, "My soul magnifies the Lord," well summarizes her response.

Though not likely educated formally, Mary's song reflects a deep knowledge of God's Word. She refers both to Abraham and quotes portions of the same song sung by the mother of Samuel. Throughout, we hear notes of humility and joy, hallmarks of Mary's life. Her life and words stand as a testament to our lives. When God is at work in our lives, we are to rejoice at being called into the service of our King.

Share your experience now at
www.ThirstNoMoreBook.com.

"The Lord's hand was with him."
—Luke 1:66

John's birth caused much excitement among his family. His father had been mute for months; His mother's pregnancy took place in her later years. She chose the name John. When his name was confirmed by the writing of Zechariah, his voice returned. Clearly, "The Lord's hand" was with this child.

They did not know John would one day baptize the Son of God. Likewise, we are unable to predict now what God will do later in our lives. All we can be certain of is God's hand at work among us now. He has chosen us, is using us, and is preparing us for future works. Let us realize God's hand is with us. Let us take confidence in His presence in our lives today.

Share your experience now at
www.ThirstNoMoreBook.com.

July 7

"I bring you good news."
—Luke 2:10

The birth of Jesus stands as one of history's most monumental moments. Yet at the time, only Joseph and Mary experienced His presence. Soon, however, angels announced the Messiah's arrival to nearby shepherds. One angel shared with those fearful at their presence, "Do not be afraid. I bring you good news that will cause great joy for all the people."

What was this "good news"? Jesus. He is the gospel. He is the joy of the angels. Still today, His life and message transform lowly shepherds and the wisest of men. It all began on a single night, in a single moment, in a single manger. Jesus was born. He was and is the good news. May we live and share Him this day.

Share your experience now at
www.ThirstNoMoreBook.com.

"A Savior has been born to you."
—Luke 2:11

Saviors are not born every day. This unique event caused angels to appear; the starry sky portrayed the locale. Prophecy had been fulfilled. In the town of David, Bethlehem, the Messiah had been born. The angel's sign was that the child would be wrapped in cloths, lying in a manger.

These exact details provided enough information to lead these unlikely fellows to the unlikely throne of the newborn King. A home for livestock held the Creator of life; simple cloths wrapped the Designer of the universe. Likewise, His life in us may not appear extravagant; however, His love in us can change hearts and nations. His Spirit in our souls can impact eternal destinies. "A Savior has been born" to us. He is Christ the Lord.

Share your experience now at
www.ThirstNoMoreBook.com.

"My eyes have seen your salvation."
—Luke 2:30

Simeon would stand as the one man who rightly recognized the infant Jesus when His parents brought Him to the temple. He had been promised he would see the Messiah before His death. Now this promise was being fulfilled. The promise was the baby in His hands.

Years later, Jesus would return again to this same locale, not for dedication but a trial for His crucifixion. But those looking for Him found Him. Those who sought Him were satisfied. The same is true today. When we seek Christ, He shows Himself to us. When we ask for Him, He answers us. Let us be among those who long to see Christ's presence at work in our lives. Let us find our only satisfaction in Him.

Share your experience now at
www.ThirstNoMoreBook.com.

"She...spoke about the child."
—Luke 2:38

Observers would guess Anna was a lonely woman. Widowed for decades, she literally lived at the temple precincts. Her life consisted of prayer and fasting, the loneliest of endeavors from a human perspective. But Anna was not alone. She walked with God.

When God appeared in the temple courts in the form of an infant, she was the one woman aside from Mary to recognize His importance. As Simeon held baby Jesus, she came forward and thanked God for this Child. Further, she spoke about Jesus to all who were looking forward to redemption. She noticed Him, praised Him, and shared His message. May we, like Anna, live in tune to with the presence of the Word made flesh, Jesus our Redeemer.

Share your experience now at
www.ThirstNoMoreBook.com.

"I had to be in my Father's house."
—Luke 2:49

Joseph and Mary had lost Jesus! Following their trip to Jerusalem, He had disappeared and been missing for three days. When they found Him, He sat asking questions of the teachers in the temple zone. The audience was amazed at His understanding and responses. But His parents were baffled: "Where have you been?"

Jesus answered, "Why were you searching? Didn't you know I had to be in my Father's house?" They did not understand the significance of His statement, but we can now. Some of these same men may have later been among those who plotted His death. On this day, they would be amazed at the young man's wisdom. Let us not simply stand amazed at Jesus; let us worship Him as God's Son.

Share your experience now at
www.ThirstNoMoreBook.com.

"Share with the one who has none."
—Luke 3:11

John preached with conviction. In fact, his crowd asked for help to apply his message of repentance. His answer? "Anyone who has two shirts should share with the one who has none." His call was not only for repentance, but for justice.

Our lives must reflect this same attitude. We are called to new life, but how does this new life look? It includes a changed heart that changes hearts. Those with two shirts share one with those without; those with extra food share with those with none. Our actions reveal our attitudes. Our reactions reflect our repentance. Our practices reveal our priorities. Changed lives change lives. Let us "share with the one who has none," for without Christ we would have nothing.

Share your experience now at
www.ThirstNoMoreBook.com.

*"He has anointed me to proclaim
good news to the poor."*
—Luke 4:18

What does it mean to be anointed? In ancient times, the practice included pouring oil over a person's head to indicate a special blessing or calling. Anointing was used for priests and kings. Jesus connected Himself as the fulfillment of prophecy, One anointed as Priest and King.

But why was He anointed? To share good news to the poor, freedom for prisoners, sight for the blind, opportunity for the oppressed, the year of the Lord's favor. These marks of the Jewish Jubilee were reasons to rejoice. Those who recognized this Anointed One did rejoice, but many missed His true purpose. Let us not be among them. Let us be among those who offer praise to Christ for His coming and His return yet to come.

Share your experience now at
www.ThirstNoMoreBook.com.

"Because you say so, I will let down the nets."
—Luke 5:5

Sometimes the requests of Christ do not make sense. There are quicker routes, more efficient alternatives, efforts we have already attempted. Simon had fished all night to no success. When Jesus asked Him to throw His nets on the opposite side of the boat, we can imagine Simon was mystified.

But because Jesus made the request, Simon Peter said yes. His obedience resulted in an enormous catch of fish. Our obedience can yield a similar response. In some situations, Jesus doesn't ask us to attempt something because it is less effective; He asks to make our faith more effective. In obeying Him, we find the greatest results. Let us obey because Jesus says so. He is the only reason we need.

Share your experience now at
www.ThirstNoMoreBook.com.

"I am a sinful man!"
—Luke 5:8

When Jesus revealed His power to Simon Peter, Simon exclaimed, "Go away from me, Lord; I am a sinful man!" His response resonates in our lives. When we experience Christ's holiness, we initially seek to flee. But Christ's response revealed His true intent: "Don't be afraid; from now on you will fish for people." Jesus did not desire fear; He desired faith.

When we come to Christ in faith, He can use us to accomplish His purposes. In Peter's case, it was a unique leadership role in the earliest Christian church. In our lives, Jesus has a unique plan that likewise requires us to move beyond fearing Christ to following Christ. Only then can we live His will. Only then will we answer His call.

Share your experience now at
www.ThirstNoMoreBook.com.

July 16

"Jesus . . . spent the night praying to God."
—Luke 6:12

When Jesus faced the difficult decision of choosing His 12 disciples, He spent an entire night in solitary prayer. If Jesus, God's Son, took the connection between decisions and intercessions so seriously, how much more do we require such meditation? Yet we often make significant choices in our own human wisdom without the slightest thought of asking God, the Giver of all wisdom.

Even if we do ask, it is often on the run or with demand for an immediate response. Such unreflective living misses the heart of our Father. He could provide an immediate answer, but often provides difficult choices to point us to His presence. Let us choose to take our burdens to Him today. He is ready to listen and answer.

Share your experience now at
www.ThirstNoMoreBook.com.

"Be merciful, just as your Father is merciful."
—Luke 6:36

A child quickly patterns his or her life after his or her Father. As we follow our heavenly Father, we reflect His ways, including His mercy. When others act wrongly or are ungrateful, He knows. Yet He also calls us to show mercy. Why? Because in doing so, we model the life of the Father.

This call is not easy or convenient, but it is right. God's way of overcoming injustice is through overwhelming justice. His way of ending hatred begins with love. His manner of increasing mercy is through increasing our mercy to others. Ultimately, our reward in heaven will be great, even if our journey on earth encounters trouble. Let us show mercy; let us reflect the heart of our Master.

Share your experience now at
www.ThirstNoMoreBook.com.

"His heart went out to her."
—Luke 7:13

Two crowds had collided. One crowd followed Jesus; another crowd traveled as a funeral procession. One walked with the only Son of God; the other walked with the only son of widow. One held the power of life; the other, the sting of death. But it was not the crowd that captured Christ's attention. It was the mother: "His heart went out to her."

First, Jesus encouraged her not to cry. Then He commanded the young man to get up. The corpse sat up! This dead man began to speak, proving he had returned to life. Both crowds stood shocked. The mother rejoiced. Remember, God sees the crowds, yet He cares for each of our specific hurts and needs. Jesus will surprise us still today.

Share your experience now at
www.ThirstNoMoreBook.com.

"A friend of tax collectors and sinners."
—Luke 7:34

Jesus was known as a friend of sinners. Unlike the religious leaders of His time, He lived among the commoners. He shared meals with those who gambled, stole, cursed, and committed a variety of other vices. His goal was never to share in their deeds; His goal was to share His new way of life.

Many continue to struggle with this idea of a God who comes to us as we are and where we are. We believe we must clean ourselves up before coming to Him, that we are not good enough to come before His presence. The truth is that we can never be good enough; that is why Jesus came to us. He desires to love us whoever and wherever we are.

Share your experience now at
www.ThirstNoMoreBook.com.

JULY 20

"I have something to tell you."
—Luke 7:40

As Jesus ate at the home of a local religious leader, a woman entered unexpectedly. Weeping, she bowed before Christ and began washing His feet with her tears. The tears were wiped with her hair, followed by perfume she had brought as a gift for the occasion.

His host believed Jesus would know who this woman was if He were really a prophet—an outcast, a sinful woman. But Jesus did not support His host; He supported His newest servant. Jesus taught those who are forgiven much would love much. Jesus then turned to the woman, saying, "Your sins are forgiven." Her faith led to action; her faith resulted in forgiveness; her forgiveness provided peace. May we love much because we have been forgiven much.

Share your experience now at
www.ThirstNoMoreBook.com.

"Tell how much God has done for you."
—Luke 8:39

Once freed from his demons, the man known as Legion now gave his allegiance to Jesus. He begged to travel with Christ, willing to serve as one of His closest followers. Instead, Jesus encouraged him to "return home and tell how much God has done for you." He did. We are left with the summary that the man spoke all over town how much Jesus had done for him.

When Christ transforms us, we sometimes expect to have some dramatic forum to spread His love. But for some of us, home is why He has changed us. Those who know us best need to know the best thing to happen to us. Let us, too, tell how much God has done for us.

Share your experience now at
www.ThirstNoMoreBook.com.

JULY 22

"Who is my neighbor?"
—Luke 10:29

To love neighbor as self requires identifying our neighbors. When Jesus was asked, "Who is my neighbor?", He did not give a definition, but a story. He spoke of a man who had been robbed, left beaten at the side of the road. Two devout Jews had spotted him but passed on the other side. But a third man, a Samaritan, stopped to help. The Samaritan was called the neighbor.

Samaritans were despised among Christ's audience. Samaritans were the least likely people they would consider acceptable neighbors. But why the Samaritan was a neighbor is the key question to answer. The reason is because he was the one "who had mercy on him." Jesus answered, "Go and do likewise." Let us show love to our neighbor today.

Share your experience now at
www.ThirstNoMoreBook.com.

"Mary has chosen what is better."
—Luke 10:42

Life is filled with choices. Many of these choices are good. How do we choose? In the case of Mary and Martha, Jesus was teaching in their own house. It would have been a thrilling event! The Son of God was sitting in their living room.

Yet there was also much work necessary to accommodate the Teacher. Of greatest importance was preparation of a proper meal. The work would require much effort, more than one person could accomplish. Martha focused on the meal. Mary focused on the Messiah. Both were important, but when Martha expressed her frustration, Jesus shared, "Mary has chosen what is better."

Are we choosing something before Christ that is good but not "better"? Remember His words. Choose Christ first.

Share your experience now at
www.ThirstNoMoreBook.com.

"Blessed rather are those who hear."
—Luke 11:28

"Blessed rather are those who hear the word of God and obey it." The teaching of Jesus regarding God's truth could not be clearer. We are to listen and live, hear and heed. Often we fall to one side or the other of this equation. At times, we are tempted to only hear God's Word, deceptively believing knowledge is enough to receive blessing.

At other times, we fall to the temptation to replace learning with doing. Action is critical, but without proper preparedness it may eventually lead to burnout and bad decisions. Only in hearing and obeying can we live as Christ intends. Let us not forget either. Jesus calls us blessed when we hear His truth and live it. Let us strive to do both today.

Share your experience now at
www.ThirstNoMoreBook.com.

"Be generous to the poor."
—Luke 11:41

There is perhaps no greater universal proof of love for God than generosity to the poor. The Pharisees, who loved power and influence, were known for their religious actions. However, Christ challenged them in their attitude toward those in physical need. His instructions? "Be generous to the poor, and everything will be clean for you."

The Pharisees were concerned with looking holy; Jesus was concerned about them living holy. Tradition was not enough; action was required. As God looks at our lives, what does He see regarding our actions toward those in need? Does He see a modern-day Pharisee or a heart overflowing with love toward the poor? Let us sees others today through the eyes of Christ. Let us be generous to the poor.

Share your experience now at
www.ThirstNoMoreBook.com.

"Be on your guard against ... hypocrisy."
—Luke 12:1

Hypocrisy hinders our journey with Christ. To say one thing yet live another strikes against everything He came to change. Hypocrisy is easy to identify in others, yet frequently difficult to spot in our own lives. How can we be on guard against it?

The answer is transparency. Transparency is to live with no secrets. When we have nothing to hide, there is nothing to hide. When those who know us see our ups and downs, they see when and where we struggle and can help us progress. It is when we seek to hide our struggles that we step toward the hypocrisy Christ warns against. Let us find friends we can live with in transparency; only then can we live on guard against hypocrisy.

Share your experience now at
www.ThirstNoMoreBook.com.

"Be on your guard against . . . greed."
—Luke 12:15

Life is more than possessions. Yet greed deceives us into believing we are what we own. Jesus warns life does not consist in an abundance of possessions. Life consists of abundant life in Him. Those who trust in their belongings belong to them. Those who identify life by their belongings are captive to their baggage.

Our Father desires better for our lives. He gives gifts because He loves us. He provides because He cares for His children. When we see His gifts as our gods, we take our eyes off of Him. In the end, we will regret such greed. This is why Christ teaches us to be on guard against greed. Let us treasure Christ, not the treasures of this earth.

Share your experience now at
www.ThirstNoMoreBook.com.

"Sell your possessions and give to the poor."
—Luke 12:33

Possessions can dominate our hearts. This is why Jesus taught us to sell our possessions and give to the poor. Whenever "things" come between us and our service to Christ, the possessions must go. Anything less is idolatry.

Jesus did not teach this because He could not provide for the poor in other ways. He commands us to part with our possessions because we often need to give up something to grow up in Him. With our resources, we help those in need. Through His resources, He meets our needs. Where our treasure is, there our heart will be also. Let us remove any possession that removes us even one step from God. Let us help those in need, just as He meets our needs.

Share your experience now at
www.ThirstNoMoreBook.com.

July 29

"Much will be demanded."
—Luke 12:48

Following one parable, Peter asked, "Was this for us or for the crowd?" Jesus answered with the words, "From everyone who has been given much, much will be demanded." Those blessed greatly must give greatly. Those changed deeply must change others deeply. We may sometimes question, "God has been so generous to me. I wonder why?" The reason is so we can serve generously.

God transforms us so we may transform others. We are not blessed so we can rest; we are blessed so we can become a blessing to others. Freely we have received; freely we give. Only when we live the Scriptures do we apply the Scriptures. Let us live not for self, but for our Savior this day.

Share your experience now at
www.ThirstNoMoreBook.com.

"Unless you repent, you too will all perish."
—Luke 13:3

In the world of Jesus, if a person's death occurred under dire conditions, it was considered judgment for their deep sinfulness. In our world, we often hear similar comments: "That person must have done something really bad to die that way." But Jesus made clear death is the same for all: "Unless you repent, you too will all perish."

The call of Jesus is to repent, to turn. As we change, Christ transforms us for His purposes. In eternity, we enjoy His perfect purpose of living in His presence. To look at death from a human perspective is not enough. We must peer with an eternal perspective into each day's events and live accordingly. Only then will we live today to its fullest.

Share your experience now at
www.ThirstNoMoreBook.com.

"You are set free from your infirmity."
—Luke 13:12

As Jesus taught in the synagogue, a crippled woman sat in the audience. For 18 years, chronic pain had forced her face toward the ground; she could not easily look up at the sun. When Jesus saw her, He called her forward: "Woman, you are set free from your infirmity." He put His hands on her, she straightened up, and praised God.

She rejoiced in her healing; but the synagogue leader rejected the healing. Why? It had taken place on a Sabbath day. He considered healing as work. Jesus rebuked the man's hypocrisy. As we reflect on our own lives, do we mimic the woman's praise or that leader's hypocrisy? Let us choose this day to look to Christ in worship, our Healer and Savior.

Share your experience now at
www.ThirstNoMoreBook.com.

AUGUST 1

"I have found my lost sheep."
—Luke 15:6

In the ancient world, if a shepherd had 100 sheep and lost 1, the expectation was to search for the lost sheep. Its discovery was a source of joy. Jesus likens this scenario to 1 person who turns to Him. There is more rejoicing in heaven over the 1 found than the 99.

Jesus is always pursuing the 1. We are each that "1" He sought to bring back to His flock. When He did, heaven rejoiced. Jesus, Creator of the universe, celebrated the day you were found. We are loved by God. May we walk in His love. May we seek those lost sheep that have yet to find their way home. When even one is found, let us rejoice with our Shepherd.

Share your experience now at
www.ThirstNoMoreBook.com.

"Rejoice with me."
—Luke 15:9

A woman with ten coins who loses one doesn't stir our hearts much. But it would if we knew the value of the lost coin. In that time, the coin used, called a drachma, equaled a day's wages. This one coin represented a full day of work. Its discovery was worth hours of searching on her behalf.

She first lit an oil lamp. She swept her home, searching every crack in its rocky floor. When she found it, she invited her neighbors over to celebrate. Likewise, "one sinner who repents" is worthy of tremendous celebration. A search has ended; rejoicing begins. Let us seek the "lost coin" in our lives today. May we rejoice with our Father at every changed life we experience.

Share your experience now at
www.ThirstNoMoreBook.com.

"He ran to his son."
—Luke 15:20

His young son had left. Alone once again, the father paced back and forth along the path in front of their home. "Will he ever return?" The son, following a time of selfish living, came to his senses. He had squandered his inheritance. Now he intended to return home a servant, no longer worthy to be called a son.

As the son approached that evening, his father spotted a figure in the distance. "Could it be? Yes, it is my son! He has come home!" Filled with compassion, the father ran to his son and threw his arms around him. The son had left, but now had returned. He was home. Our Father runs to us, arms open. Let us embrace His love this day.

Share your experience now at
www.ThirstNoMoreBook.com.

"God knows your hearts."
—Luke 16:15

When Jesus taught a person cannot serve both God and money, the Pharisees sneered at Him. His response? "God knows your hearts." These words resonate through the generations into our lives today. God knows our every thought and desire. Nothing is hidden before Him.

We wrongly believe we can hide from God or choose to reveal only part of our lives to Him. But God sees our every longing. Our only genuine response is to confess our flaws and depend on His mercy for help. He desires our lives to be focused on Him. As we do, He views our spirit and is pleased with what He sees: "God knows your hearts." Let Him see in us a heart turned fully toward Him this day.

Share your experience now at
www.ThirstNoMoreBook.com.

"We have only done our duty."
—Luke 17:10

When God uses us, the temptation is to take credit for His enablement. The glory due to Christ can be taken upon ourselves. Yet there is another way. In Christ's teachings, He shares a scene in which a servant prepares a meal for his master at the end of a long day of work. As Jesus illustrates, preparing such a meal is not a reason to draw attention; rather, it is simply part of fulfilling our duty.

In the end, our expression must be, "We are unworthy servants; we have only done our duty." Christ calls and provides. We are but His workers, His laborers of choice to accomplish His will. As we better understand our role, we better comprehend His role as our Master.

Share your experience now at
www.ThirstNoMoreBook.com.

"Jesus, Master, have pity on us!"
—Luke 17:13

Ten men with leprosy met Jesus outside of a village. Unable to enter their own community due to disease, they could only catch His attention from a distance before Jesus entered the area. Their wish? "Jesus, Master, have pity on us!"

Rather than heal them immediately, Jesus sent them to the priests. This command implied healing would come, as a priest was required to declare a leprous person clean before he could return to their home. As they walked, their disease disappeared. They were clean. Only one returned to praise God—a foreigner. Jesus commended his response, rare in His time and ours. May we respond as he did, praising Christ for our healed lives. May we rejoice in His work within us this day.

Share your experience now at
www.ThirstNoMoreBook.com.

"He will see that they get justice."
—Luke 18:8

A widow ranked as a position of lowliness in ancient society. A judge stood as a position of influence. Jesus spoke of one widow who persistently advocated for her community's judge to provide justice for her against her adversary. The judge initially refused, yet later answered to stop the woman's pleading.

Jesus used this story to highlight the infinitely greater concerns of our God. When His people cry out against injustice, He hears and responds. When we call to Him, He will come to us. We need not fear He will not hear or answer. Our Father loves us and has our best in mind. Let us come to Him with our petitions and daily needs. He wants to see that we receive justice.

Share your experience now at
www.ThirstNoMoreBook.com.

August 8

"God, have mercy on me, a sinner."
—Luke 18:13

Two men; two responses. One a religious man; one branded a sinner. We would expect the religious man to stand justified before God. But Jesus offers the unexpected. The sinful tax collector is presented as the one God desires. Why? He did not justify himself; he begged for mercy.

"Those who exalt themselves will be humbled," declares Jesus. When we list our good deeds before Him, we only reveal our deep need to see Him more clearly. Only when we humble ourselves and ask for mercy do we identify as we should. Only when we see ourselves as sinners in need of His grace can we experience the justification He provides. Let us not boast of our deeds; let us approach Him on our knees.

Share your experience now at
www.ThirstNoMoreBook.com.

"Today salvation has come to this house."
—Luke 19:9

Zacchaeus sought Jesus. A short man, Zacchaeus climbed a nearby tree to spot Jesus as He passed through the crowd. Surprising Zacchaeus, Jesus paused below this particular tree to call him: "Zacchaeus, come down immediately. I must stay at your house today." When Zacchaeus sought, Jesus stopped.

Jesus still operates in this way. When we seek, He stops. He calls us to follow Him. His desire is to commune with us. Why? For the same reason He called Zacchaeus in that ancient time. Jesus longs to seek and save the lost. Sinners do not cause Jesus to run; they cause Him to respond. He longs to spend time with the true children of God. Seek Him today; then answer His call to deeper, abiding relationship.

Share your experience now at
www.ThirstNoMoreBook.com.

AUGUST 10

"If they keep quiet, the stones will cry out."
—Luke 19:40

When Jesus entered Jerusalem, crowds revered Him. Spreading their coats on the road for Him to pass over, they acknowledged their desire for Jesus as the coming King. The Pharisees watched in fury: "Teacher, rebuke your disciples!" They refused to accept Him as anyone more than another Rabbi. Their goal was to end the celebration.

Jesus answered, "If they keep quiet, the stones will cry out." Why these words? Referring to a prophecy these Pharisees would know, He subtly communicated His role as coming One. These leaders looked into the eyes of the Messiah and rejected Him. As we walk in His presence this day, do our lives reflect a rejection of our Messiah, or a celebration? Let us worship Him anew, Christ the Lord.

Share your experience now at
www.ThirstNoMoreBook.com.

"He wept over it."
—Luke 19:41

The crowd rejoiced as Jesus approached the city; Jesus wept over it. Why? Jesus knew what would one day happen to this leading city. They would soon reject Him as Messiah. In the days to follow, the city would be devastated by its enemies. Many would die; there would be much suffering. At the thought of this impending doom, Jesus wept.

Jesus could have wept over what would happen to Him a few days later. Instead, His heart ached in compassion for people. His compassion stands as a model for us. Rather than focus on the struggles of our own lives, let our hearts be broken by what breaks the heart of God. Then through our actions, we will reflect the heart of Christ.

Share your experience now at
www.ThirstNoMoreBook.com.

"All the people hung on his words."
—Luke 19:48

What would it have been like to listen to Jesus teach? Scripture records He was so powerful that those opposed had trouble killing Him because "all the people hung on his words." His words offered hope and life. Those who listened and responded were transformed, changed.

This contrast between those who oppose Christ and those who hang on His words endures still. We either oppose Him or cling to His words. We cannot do both. Our inaction stands as action opposed to His teachings. Our neglect notes our negativity to His ways. May we recall past times when His Word came alive; let us strive to reconnect in this way again today. Let us hang on His words, the words of life.

Share your experience now at
www.ThirstNoMoreBook.com.

August 13

"Who gave you this authority?"
—Luke 20:2

As Jesus taught in the temple courts, the religious teachers challenged Him once again: "Who gave you this authority?" Rather than answer directly, Jesus responded with His own question about John the Baptist. His goal? To reveal their true fear. These men did not fear God; they feared people.

Even the most religious person can struggle with seeking the approval of others. Yet Jesus spoke to please the Father. As we follow His example, we find our views controversial at times. Others will not always appreciate our views or actions. We must not falter, but have faith. Christ has not called us to be popular, but to be faithful. We are not saved to be relevant to the crowds; we are saved to reflect Christ.

Share your experience now at
www.ThirstNoMoreBook.com.

AUGUST 14

"Give ... to God what is God's."
—Luke 20:25

Spies pressed Jesus for an answer they could use to arrest Him. Their plan? Conspiracy against the government: "Is it right for us to pay taxes to Caesar or not?" Jesus knew their true intentions. He asked for a coin, instructing them to give back to Caesar what is his, and to "give to God what is God's."

Similarly, we sometimes attempt to "trick" Jesus into saying something we can use for our own desires. Rather than seek what His Word teaches, we seek loopholes in Scripture to justify our selfish actions. But our goal cannot be to move as close to sin as possible; it must be to move closer to our Savior. Our pursuit must not be pride; it must be His presence.

Share your experience now at
www.ThirstNoMoreBook.com.

"Be careful, or your hearts will be weighed down."
—Luke 21:34

When Jesus spoke of His future coming, He warned, "Be careful, or your hearts will be weighed down." His concern is many will live for self-fulfillment, personal pleasure, or the stresses of life, only to find themselves surprised in the end. If we honestly reflect on our own lives, we would all admit we are guilty to some degree.

Jesus provides these words to point us toward holiness now, not just in heaven. He desires us to live sacred, set apart, free from the control of possessions and addictions. If our lives are to truly please Him, we must acknowledge our temptation to focus on the temporary and away from the eternal. Only then will we "be careful" to keep proper priorities for His coming.

Share your experience now at
www.ThirstNoMoreBook.com.

"Do this in remembrance of me."
—Luke 22:19

When the disciples ate with Jesus the night of His arrest, they did could not imagine what would soon take place. It was a special meal for Passover, not their intention to begin a new pattern for God's people. What was simply bread and wine would soon become the ceremony used by many.

Do we, like the disciples, find ourselves overlooking the importance of ordinary moments? Is Jesus beginning something new in us we are failing to notice? As we remember the final meal of Jesus with His disciples, let us consider the voice of Jesus to us this day. Let us not live in routine without reflection; let us consider what our Master desires to share with us in this moment.

Share your experience now at
www.ThirstNoMoreBook.com.

"I am among you as one who serves."
—Luke 22:27

On Christ's final night with His followers, He could confidently share, "I am among you as one who serves." This powerful truth reveals two insights for our journey with Him. First, Jesus lived among those He served. He did not operate as a King separated from His subjects, but lived day and night with His followers.

Second, Jesus served. Ultimately, He would serve by dying to redeem us. These two insights—living among others and serving others—must be embraced by all who seek to pattern themselves after Christ. We can impress others from a distance, but we impact others up close. We transform the life of another by serving, not demanding service. Let us seek to apply these traits of our Savior today.

Share your experience now at
www.ThirstNoMoreBook.com.

"The whole assembly . . . led him off to Pilate."
—Luke 23:1

The Jewish leaders had no authority to put a criminal to death—but Pilate did. In their plot to murder Jesus, they accused Him of subversion, opposing taxes, and claiming to be a king. They were only right on one account: Jesus did claim to be King. But the kingdom He claimed to lead was not of this world. He spoke of something enduring, eternal.

His opponents could only see what was now. We find ourselves guilty of this same spiritual blindness. We seek convenience, comfort, and answer to every consideration for our benefit— now. In doing so, we find ourselves resembling Christ's enemies rather than Christ Himself. He endured suffering on earth to change lives for eternity. May we live with His perspective today.

Share your experience now at
www.ThirstNoMoreBook.com.

"What crime has this man committed?"
—Luke 23:22

On three occasions, Pilate sought to free Jesus. In his final plea, he asked His accusers, "Why? What crime has this man committed?" Pilate had found no reason to sentence Jesus to the death penalty. Jesus was innocent. He was the spotless Lamb sacrificed on our behalf. He lived without blemish and without sin in a world where sin pervades every aspect of our lives.

We easily forget Jesus was not only wrongfully punished, but He was also wrongfully accused. His enemies presented false claims against the true Christ. They spewed lies against the One called "the Truth." In our lives, let us likewise stand pure when others speak critically of us. Only then do we model the way of our Master.

Share your experience now at
www.ThirstNoMoreBook.com.

AUGUST 20

"Father, forgive them,
for they know not what they are doing."
—Luke 23:34

When Jesus was crucified, He did not retaliate. Instead, He prayed for His executors. Jesus did not only teach to pray for those who persecute you; He lived it. The One with the power to raise the dead allowed His life to be taken, even praying, "Father, forgive them, for they know not what they are doing."

This same love and forgiveness extends to us now. If Jesus can pray for those who crucified Him, He can also intercede to the Father for us. When we do not know what to pray, we must only come to Him. Words are not necessary. Christ will spread out His hands before the Father, revealing His nail-scarred hands, and say on our behalf, "Father, forgive them."

Share your experience now at
www.ThirstNoMoreBook.com.

"Jesus, remember me."
—Luke 23:42

Jesus did not die alone on the Cross. Two criminals hung that day as well. At first they mocked Him along with the crowd. But at some point, one of these men reconsidered. Defending Jesus to the other criminal, He made clear His belief Jesus had done nothing deserving of death.

Instead, this dying soul humbled Himself: "Jesus, remember me when you come into your kingdom." Jesus promised this man He would be with him in paradise—today! This lawbreaker could never prove his repentance through his good deeds; he would never be baptized. Yet Jesus promised him eternity with Him. Why? Because entry to the kingdom is not based on our efforts, but through Christ's effort on the Cross. Let us cry out likewise, "Jesus, remember me!"

Share your experience now at
www.ThirstNoMoreBook.com.

"Then they remembered his words."
—Luke 24:8

Seeing is believing. Sometimes seeing is also remembering. When the women heard the message of the angels at the tomb of Jesus, Scripture shares, "Then they remembered his words." Jesus had predicted His death and crucifixion, but His closest followers did not understand. When they saw the empty tomb, they remembered.

Our lives often reflect this principle. We know the truth of Christ, but only remember when we experience it. We understand the power of prayer, yet only remember when we pray. We know the power of serving Christ, but fail to comprehend until we practice it. Today God may not be calling us to learn more, but to remember more. Let us live His truth and remember the power of Christ this day.

Share your experience now at
www.ThirstNoMoreBook.com.

"Were not our hearts burning within us?"
—Luke 24:32

On the day of the Resurrection, Jesus walked with two men to Emmaus. Little did they know, they were among the first to experience the risen Christ. As day turned to evening, they invited Him to share a meal. When He prayed, they recognized Him. After His departure, they asked one another, "Were not our hearts burning within us while he talked with us on the road and opened the Scriptures to us?"

Christ speaks to us through Scripture. There, our hearts burn as we ponder God's truth. There is no substitute for His words in our lives. If we lack fire in our daily existence, it may be due to neglecting the flames of Scripture. Let us be warmed by His words this day.

Share your experience now at
www.ThirstNoMoreBook.com.

"Touch me and see."
—Luke 24:39

When the risen Lord appeared, His disciples stood in fear. Their initial reaction was He was some sort of spirit. But Jesus provided two facts of His physical return to life. First, he challenged His followers to touch Him. They could feel the scars on His feet and hands.

Second, Jesus ate before them. Only a person with a real body would consume food. Some speculate Jesus only returned spiritually, but Jesus was clear He had returned with beating heart, skin, and even scars. He did not merely exist as spirit after death; He conquered death. Whatever our weaknesses or doubts, we can live in the power of the One who defeated death. Nothing is too difficult for us today; His power lives in us.

Share your experience now at
www.ThirstNoMoreBook.com.

"He lifted up his hands and blessed them."
—Luke 24:50

Jesus returned, but only for a short time. He proved He had conquered the grave; now He would return to God. To commemorate His ascension, He left His followers with a parting gift—His blessing. We are not told the content of His blessing; only that He lifted up His hand and blessed them. His final words were those of encouragement.

In His time on earth, our Lord spoke words of wisdom, judgment, healing, and mystery. Yet He reserved in His parting words a moment to lift up before He was lifted up. We often underestimate the power of our words. He has given us the message of life. Let us use our voices to encourage the hurting, reflecting the example of our risen Christ.

Share your experience now at
www.ThirstNoMoreBook.com.

"Then they worshiped him."
—Luke 24:52

Jesus ascended; His followers worshipped. This tradition has become our tradition. As we await His return, we praise His name, for He has defeated death and the grave. Worship is sometimes associated with songs, prayers, or buildings. But we see in these words that worship is ultimately a response. Christ has changed us; our response is to return thanks, to worship Him.

Those who walked with Him on earth model the way for us. As we experience the risen Lord, we enter His presence with great joy, with worship, and with praise. We dare not live discouraged; we live delighted as we reflect on our coming King. Until His return, let us continually worship Christ, our risen Master and Messiah.

Share your experience now at
www.ThirstNoMoreBook.com.

"In the beginning was the Word."
—John 1:1

The first words of Genesis echo in the first words of John's Gospel: "In the beginning…" But what was in the beginning? God. John reveals this God consisted of both God the Father and the Word, Jesus Christ. Jesus did not recently appear; He had existed from eternity past with the Father.

The human temptation is to make Jesus simply human. Though He lived among us as fully man, He is also fully God. When we look to Him, we do not only see a great moral teacher; we look upon the Maker of the universe, the Maker of our very world and souls. Jesus has existed from eternity past with us in mind. Let us worship Him this day as eternal God.

Share your experience now at
www.ThirstNoMoreBook.com.

"The Word was with God."
—John 1:1

Jesus did not exist alone in the beginning. He was with God. He came to live with us as Immanuel, yet He was with God in the beginning. Jesus is eternal; He is also communal. Within the Triune God of Father, Son, and Spirit, there is relationship at a level mysterious to humanity. Yet we do know for certain that within God Himself is a perfect reflection of community.

This community extends to us. Through Jesus, we receive access to the Father. The Holy Spirit lives within us. We also experience community with all God's children who know Christ. How blessed we are! We can intimately connect with our Creator and His people because of Jesus. Let live aware of this blessing each moment today.

Share your experience now at
www.ThirstNoMoreBook.com.

"The Word was God."
—John 1:1

The defining line of our faith is that Jesus is God. No alternative view is possible for those who claim the name "Christian." He was not a god or like God; He is God. John made this clear from the first words of his message. He had no desire to be unclear in His message. He had every desire to present Jesus as God among us.

Many views exist of Jesus in our world; to connect with Christ, we must accept Him as Christ. He offers a relationship unmatched; it is an intimacy impossible elsewhere. We must only come to Him on His terms, not our own. We cannot make Jesus in our likeness, but must rather conform to His likeness. Let us worship Him alone. Jesus is God.

Share your experience now at
www.ThirstNoMoreBook.com.

AUGUST 30

"Through him all things were made."
—John 1:3

We are created by God. More specifically, we are made "through" Christ. Every person who has ever lived is the result of His craftsmanship. Why is this important? What God makes is good. Though flawed and weak, we are created in His image. He has designed us; He loves us.

So often, we base our worth on the opinions of others. But they do not own us, did not create us, nor do they usually know us intimately. But Christ does. He created us for His purposes, to further His glory. There is nothing we could ever do to make Him love us more; there is nothing we can do to make Him love us less. Let us live in the confidence of His love today.

Share your experience now at
www.ThirstNoMoreBook.com.

"In him was life."
—John 1:4

When John speaks of life, he does not always make clear whether he speaks of physical or spiritual life. Though aware of the differences, he often blurred these distinctives. In his mind, Jesus was the maker of our physical bodies and our souls.

Our modern world encourages us to make spirituality one aspect of our lives. Like one spoke on a wheel, faith has its place, similar to a hobby or physical fitness. But these words make clear our soul is not secondary. Faith dominates life. Our soul must be given attention, being nurtured in order to fully develop the life God has given us. Let us not neglect this gift of life. Let us live devoted to our Creator.

Share your experience now at
www.ThirstNoMoreBook.com.

September 1

"The light shines in the darkness."
—John 1:5

Light is the opposite of dark. Jesus is the opposite of evil. He is perfect God, offering light to all who embrace Him. Other realities may offers some light or escape some darkness, but they are not the light. Only Jesus can satisfy the soul; only Christ can quench our thirst.

Yet how often we live as if other pursuits satisfy! The latest trend, human relationship, or project all compete for our allegiance. Interruptions pursue the cracks of time Jesus desires to fill with His presence. Let us not seek ultimate satisfaction in other endeavors; we will certainly be disappointed. May we find satisfaction in His light, where He provides warmth and light for the struggles of life: "The light shines in the darkness."

Share your experience now at
www.ThirstNoMoreBook.com.

"The right to become children of God."
—John 1:12

How do we become children of God? Believe and receive. We believe in Jesus as God's Son; we receive Him as Savior of our lives. Unlike any other family relationship, our status before God is birthed through faith, not law or biology. We must come to Him to be born in Him.

To be born of God is the greatest of all births. Every person is born once; only those who trust in the eternal-life Giver can be born a second time. Our Father is no longer an earthly one, whether positive or negative; our Father is a heavenly one, perfect in all ways. In His arms, we need not fear. We need only stay close to Him; He will care for us, His children.

Share your experience now at
www.ThirstNoMoreBook.com.

SEPTEMBER 2

"The right to become children of God."
—John 1:12

How do we become children of God? Believe and receive. We believe in Jesus as God's Son; we receive Him as Savior of our lives. Unlike any other family relationship, our status before God is birthed through faith, not law or biology. We must come to Him to be born in Him.

To be born of God is the greatest of all births. Every person is born once; only those who trust in the eternal-life Giver can be born a second time. Our Father is no longer an earthly one, whether positive or negative; our Father is a heavenly one, perfect in all ways. In His arms, we need not fear. We need only stay close to Him; He will care for us, His children.

Share your experience now at
www.ThirstNoMoreBook.com.

"The Word became flesh."
—John 1:14

Jesus became human. He had existed from eternity past; He later took the form of a physical body in a lowly manger in Bethlehem. Rather than reign from the heavens, He chose to serve from the earth. His plan required a limitation upon Himself to remove our limitations. Our redemption required His revelation.

We often see the baby Jesus as the story of an infant's beginning. It is much more. Jesus began His earthly life by leaving His heavenly glory. His mission required becoming human. Still today, our Lord seeks to become personal to each moment of our lives. Let us meditate upon His guiding presence within us; let us live with power through us.

Share your experience now at
www.ThirstNoMoreBook.com.

"And made his dwelling among us."
—John 1:14

The phrase "made his dwelling among us" include the idea of Jesus setting up His tent (so to speak) among us. He came to enter into our journey; not merely direct it. By dwelling among us, He modeled the life He desires for us while accomplishing His eternal plan of redemption. When we see Him, we see patterns to copy. When we observe His actions, we discover attitudes to apply.

None of this would be available unless He had dwelt among us. God came near to show the way. Like a light, He guides us to the desires of the Father, the heart of our Maker. Through Him, we know the will of our Master. Let us model the life of Christ as we dwell among others.

Share your experience now at
www.ThirstNoMoreBook.com.

"Grace and truth came through Jesus Christ."
—John 1:17

The Law came through Moses. Grace and truth, through Jesus. Why couldn't Moses have provided grace and truth? He was human. Though God's servant, He was not perfect. Another would be required. Grace is God's favor, something He alone can grant. Truth is an attribute of God's personality. He revealed it personally through His Son, Jesus.

We often believe we can provide the changes our world or our loved ones need. If we work enough, pray enough, last long enough, won't that be enough? But it is only God who can extend His grace. Only God can open eyes to truth. We can live as conduits of our Lord, but He must be the One to bring grace and truth. Let us live in the grace we have received. Let us live the truth we have been given.

Share your experience now at
www.ThirstNoMoreBook.com.

"Look, the Lamb of God."
—John 1:29

When John saw Jesus, he called Him the "Lamb of God." Why? First, a lamb was considered pure, white as snow. Second, a lamb was required according to Jewish custom as a sacrifice for sin. John declared this was the One who would take away the sin of the world. In John's words, "This is the one I meant."

One neglected aspect of Jesus is His role as our atonement for sin. He forgives our sin because He was sacrificed in place of our sin. We do not need to bring a lamb or die for our transgressions. We instead need only to look to Jesus. He is the One, the Lamb of God. He came to take away our sin.

Share your experience now at
www.ThirstNoMoreBook.com.

"We have found the Messiah."
—John 1:41

Jesus calls us to call others. Andrew was one of the first two followers of Christ. We are told "the first thing" Andrew did was to find his brother to share, "We have found the Messiah." Not willing to stop with sharing, Andrew took his brother to Jesus.

We are fully aware of our responsibility to share the Christ we serve. But are we urgent in our response? Are we willing to make speaking of Christ our "first thing"? Do we seek to bring others into His midst? Andrew not only shared the message; he took his brother directly to Jesus. We must likewise make speaking of Jesus a high priority, taking all we can directly to our Lord's presence.

Share your experience now at
www.ThirstNoMoreBook.com.

"Come and see."
—John 1:46

When we invite others to Jesus, we invite them to experience Him. Jesus requires much, but the invitation begins with an introduction. As we speak of our Lord, our priority is not rules and regulations, but an appeal to relationship. Only in knowing Him does His call to "Follow Me" make sense. Only in encountering Christ does embracing His way stand as the only option.

Perhaps we have personally forgotten the truth that knowing Christ is a "come and see" experience. If our souls feel dry and empty, we may need to come to Him afresh, looking to Him rather than to our obligations. He longs to commune with us moment by moment. Let us accept His call this day to "come and see."

Share your experience now at
www.ThirstNoMoreBook.com.

"Do whatever he tells you."
—John 2:5

More than anyone, Mary lived keenly aware of her Son's uniqueness. When there was a problem, she could turn to Him for the answer. So when the wedding she was attending ran out of wine, she brought Jesus to the servants, instructing, "Do whatever he tells you."

In their case, they experienced a miracle. But we overlook that they did not realize at the time what was about to happen. They simply obeyed orders. Likewise, we know not when Christ intends to act in a supernatural way among us. We are called to obey. Let us live for Him with renewed vigor, living fully aware that He may perform a miracle among us at any moment today. Let us do whatever He tells us.

Share your experience now at
www.ThirstNoMoreBook.com.

"He revealed his glory."
—John 2:11

Miracles exist for God's glory. When we ask for miracles, we often do so for our own purposes. When we see a miracle, we likewise tend to accept credit or explain the supernatural as other than God. Yet God's purpose in providing such signs is to point to Him. Any other response is less than His desire.

When He performed His first sign, Christ's disciples believed in Him. God's glory inspires deeper belief. Regardless of how we feel at the moment, let us reflect on the glory of God. As we do, may we remember His miracles in days past; may we deepen our faith; may we look forward to how God works today to further bring glory to His name.

Share your experience now at
www.ThirstNoMoreBook.com.

"Your miraculous signs are evidence that God is with you."
—John 3:2 (NLT)

Nicodemus was a leader. He recognized other leaders by their similar influence. In the case of Jesus, Nicodemus knew He was more than a gifted orator or organizer. Jesus walked with a divine touch.

In curiosity, Nicodemus sought out Jesus to discover more. Jesus offered Him not words, but an invitation—"You must be born again."

Rebirth, not curiosity, was Christ's goal. His call to us is the same. Be changed. Be transformed. Be reborn.

Do not be satisfied with your fascination for Jesus; He longs for your heart. Nicodemus knew God's Scriptures; what he lacked was an experience with God's Son.

Christ calls you not only to seek Him, but to savor Him. To rest in Him. To find your life, new life.

Share your experience now at
www.ThirstNoMoreBook.com.

"Unless they are born again."
—John 3:3

Access to the kingdom is not automatic. Jesus clearly stated the requirement to the kingdom of God: "No one can see the kingdom of God unless they are born again." Nicodemus, a religious leader, struggled to understand this statement. Why a second birth?

Birth represents life. Jesus taught the way to the kingdom was through new life. This life Nicodemus sought to understand stood before him that night. New life is not found within us; it is found in Christ. Let us not fall for the temptation to believe our efforts earn us the right to the kingdom; only God's grace is sufficient. We are saved to serve, but without salvation, we are without hope. We must be born again.

Share your experience now at
www.ThirstNoMoreBook.com.

"God so loved the world."
—John 3:16

The most famous words in Scripture reflect one of God's most famous truths: "God so loved the world." In these words we find all of life. God. Love. World. Him. His way. Us. Only in God is truest love found. Only in love is God found. Only in God do we find divine love.

God created us for His purposes. We do not need to live without hope in this world; we have the hope of the world within us! Our lives here are but a temporary pilgrimage toward the eternal destination of eternity with Christ. Today's troubles may cause us great pain now, but they cannot hurt us beyond this world. We will live in His presence forever. Let us live aware of His presence now.

Share your experience now at
www.ThirstNoMoreBook.com.

"Whoever believes in him."
—John 3:16

Not all souls enter heaven, but all are given opportunity for eternal life. This majestic truth brings joy to those excluded from the privileges of this world: "whoever believes in him" To be included removes insecurity, instability, and doubt in a world where humanity competes in every conceivable category. In God's kingdom, there is no competition; there is compassion.

Our challenge in this life is to shower similar compassion on our fellow pilgrims whenever possible. We still tend to compete, either standing one step higher or lower than the next person. But in Christ, we are compelled to extend His touch to include the outcast of our communities, to love as He loves, to offer hope to all who will receive it.

Share your experience now at
www.ThirstNoMoreBook.com.

"Whoever believes in him shall not perish."
—John 3:16

This world is not all there is. If there were no hope beyond this life, our lives would be pitiful indeed. Jesus addresses this fear with an offer of life—eternal life. We who believe in Him will not perish. Our bodies may fade away, but we will live.

The human fear of mortality runs deep. We often strive for any pursuit to prolong life, health, and youthful vigor. But God encourages us to embrace this life as but preparation for the next. In Him, our limitations become a source for His limitless power to renew in the life to come. He is our eternal Father. He, too, looks forward to the day when we dwell in His presence for eternity.

Share your experience now at
www.ThirstNoMoreBook.com.

"Whoever believes in him is not condemned."
—John 3:18

Do you feel rejected? Discouraged? Christ knows our feelings; He has responded already through the words He has revealed to us. In His conversation with Nicodemus, Jesus shared words likely comforting to him: "Whoever believes in him is not condemned." Nicodemus could have been condemned for befriending Jesus; many of us are condemned for various reasons. But Jesus encourages us: condemnation need not endure.

In Christ, rejection has been replaced with relief; pain has been exchanged for peace. Yes, in this world we will have trouble. But we also have Christ. In His presence is acceptance. We do not need to perform nor impress Him. He loves us as we are. When we believe, condemnation is completely removed. We are loved completely in Christ.

Share your experience now at
www.ThirstNoMoreBook.com.

September 17

"He must become greater."
—John 3:30

John's disciples viewed Christ's success as competition. More people were turning to Jesus for baptism. What should they do? John's words reflect a clear understanding of his calling. He knew both his role and the role of the Messiah: "He must become greater; I must become less."

Apart from Christ, we can do nothing. With Christ, we can do what He enables us to accomplish. Our proper response is humility. He calls, He empowers, He receives the glory. When others find success in serving Christ, we can celebrate their impact. When others overlook our efforts, we need not cry out for attention. Our effort is to honor Christ. If He receives glory, that is all that matters: "He must become greater."

Share your experience now at
www.ThirstNoMoreBook.com.

"He would have given you living water."
—John 4:10

Christ's conversation with the woman at the well speaks volumes. The woman understands the tension between their two peoples. What she does not understand is the power of the One asking her for a drink. If she did, Jesus said, she would have asked for living water. She would thirst no more.

We, likewise, often misunderstand the Christ who reveals Himself to us. We see Him as someone to please. Jesus offers living water. We view Him as another task requiring energy. He offers to quench our thirst. Let us see Christ for who He is; not a self-centered taker, but the Giver of life. He is available to offer a drink to our weary souls. Let us desire His living water.

Share your experience now at
www.ThirstNoMoreBook.com.

"Whoever drinks the water I give."
—John 4:14

Our temptation is to view God's blessing as temporary. We seek Him in times of trouble or experience Him in a time of refreshing, yet later resort to life in our own strength. We look with envy on the few individuals who appear to walk close to God day after day, dreaming of such ability, but not really expecting it in our own lives.

But Jesus offers living water! "Whoever drinks the water I give them will never thirst." He has given us the capacity to walk hand in hand with Him daily. We may not always make use of this privilege, but Jesus remains available to comfort, to guide, and to quench our thirst. Let us return to our Living Water and find fulfillment in Him.

Share your experience now at
www.ThirstNoMoreBook.com.

"I can see that you are a prophet."
—John 4:19

When Jesus begins to reveal Himself, the human temptations is to make Him special, but not Savior. Countless individuals throughout the ages have spoken of Jesus as rabbi, healer, or prophet, but Jesus demands something more.

The woman at the well stood amazed at His knowledge of her personal life. She saw Him at this point as prophet. As such, her next question spoke to one of her spiritual questions regarding worship. He answered, but pressed on until she realized His desire was for her to acknowledge Him as Messiah, not simply a prophet. Let us not view Jesus as merely someone special—He is God. Let us worship Him in words and actions. Let us not seek Him as prophet; let us seek His presence.

Share your experience now at
www.ThirstNoMoreBook.com.

"Because of the woman's testimony."
—John 4:39

She had experienced Jesus; then she shared her experience. A woman who snuck out to draw water in the heat of day now walked back to town to initiate conversation. Many believed "because of the woman's testimony."

We often underestimate our influence in sharing our experience of Jesus. We fear rejection, either of our message or ourselves. But those who share stories of God's grace are those who see God's grace multiplied in others. If this one woman had not shared her story, an entire town would have missed out on Jesus. Who might miss out if we do not share our story? Let us not find out; let us speak of His change in our lives to all who will listen.

Share your experience now at
www.ThirstNoMoreBook.com.

"Pick up your mat and walk."
—John 5:8

What should a person do when given the option of obeying Christ's command or religious tradition? Choose Jesus. When one crippled man talked with Jesus on the Sabbath, he was commanded, "Get up! Pick up your mat and walk." He did and was healed. But this day was also the Sabbath. He had violated their law.

What if this man had strictly obeyed tradition? Would he have been healed that day? We do not know. What we do know is his story has been shared for our learning. We are each called by Christ to obey in some area of life. Are we willing to do it? Now? Let us say yes to Jesus. Let us get up, pick up our mats (so to speak), and walk.

Share your experience now at
www.ThirstNoMoreBook.com.

"I seek not to please myself."
—John 5:30

Jesus did not seek to please Himself. His singular goal was to follow God's plan. Many did not understand His mission. He did not come to reign as king in His first coming; He came to realize the Father's will.

His mission serves as model for ours. Our human inclination struggles for priority, position, and prestige. Yet Jesus exemplifies a life devoted to the Father's will. Only then will we find fulfillment. All other pursuits are futile; all other efforts a path to failure and frustration. The Father's will is the way. We must seek to please Him; in Him we find our source of satisfaction. The Son points toward the Father; may our lives point to Him as well.

Share your experience now at
www.ThirstNoMoreBook.com.

"If you believed Moses, you would believe me."
—John 5:46

The Pharisees lived by the Law—the Law of Moses. Yet Jesus claimed they did not believe Moses. These religious leaders would have been infuriated at this accusation. How could He claim they did not believe Moses?

Jesus claimed they did not believe Moses because Moses spoke of Him. If they rejected Jesus, they didn't acknowledge Moses as true. Jesus is the fulfillment of the Law. When we accept Him, we accept His revelation as true. We may never fully understand His Word, but we believe in it, just as we believe in Him. Let us honor His revealed truth; let us live the words of the living Christ. He is the Word, the author of knowledge and eternal life.

Share your experience now at
www.ThirstNoMoreBook.com.

"Believe in the one he has sent."
—John 6:29

Those who seek to please God ask, "What must we do?" Christ offered a puzzling response to His seekers: "The work of God is this: to believe in the one he has sent." Belief is action. Many misunderstood, expecting to perform certain deeds. But Christ's way is faith. Faith leads to action, but faith also is the response He desires.

Our humanity continues to struggle with faith as action. We separate faith from our deeds as if one is distinct from the other. Yet Christlike action is impossible apart from faith in Christ. We must believe to please Him. Then, our actions will serve as a response to faith, not a substitute for it. Let us believe and walk in light of this belief.

Share your experience now at
www.ThirstNoMoreBook.com.

"I am the bread of life."
—John 6:35

Bread is required because we hunger. In declaring Himself the Bread of life, Jesus chose a metaphor that exchanges the Holy One with our fulfillment of hunger. He had fed the crowds bread in the wilderness to fulfill hunger; now He spoke of bread that prevented hunger for eternity. This deep connection with everyday life certainly spoke deeply to His audience, including many who struggled for their daily food needs.

In our relative abundance, we can easily underestimate the importance of Jesus as Bread of life. Without food, we hunger, then die. Apart from Christ, our souls hunger and eventually perish. We cannot survive without Christ. Let us draw near to Him today; let us call to Him as our Bread of life.

Share your experience now at
www.ThirstNoMoreBook.com.

"Unless the Father who sent me draws them."
—John 6:44

Early in our faith, we believe we saw our need for salvation and responded to the call of Christ. As we grow, we realize a startling reality—we would never come to Christ unless He had first drawn us to Him. Our human nature longs for more, but seeks to fulfill through selfish pursuits. Only God could direct to His grace.

This same God who draws us to Him will raise us up with Him in the end. We need not fear whether we will endure. The One who has called us will sustain us. Our Savior provides for every facet of our salvation from beginning to end. We need only to stay in step with His will, knowing He guides us along the path.

Share your experience now at
www.ThirstNoMoreBook.com.

SEPTEMBER 28

"The Spirit gives life."
—John 6:63

The Spirit gives life. We live in this life, but we cannot provide it. We share it, but we cannot create it. God alone chooses and saves those He desires. Jesus experienced this issue among His own followers. One of His closest servants would later betray Him to death. Proximity to Jesus is not enough; only the Spirit gives life.

We are sometimes surprised when a person who has spent years in church turns against Jesus. There may be a variety of reasons for this, but we should not be shocked. Apart from His Spirit within us, we too would betray our Savior. Let us thank God for His Spirit within us. Let us follow its leading today, not our own: "The Spirit gives life."

Share your experience now at
www.ThirstNoMoreBook.com.

"Lord, to whom shall we go?"
—John 6:68

At one point, many of Christ's early followers abandoned Him. Turning to the Twelve, He asked, "You do not want to leave too, do you?" Simon Peter answered, "Lord, to whom shall we go? You have the words of eternal life." Following Christ is a struggle at times. But there is no better way to struggle than in His service.

As Peter noted, is there anywhere else more satisfying? Only Christ holds the words of life. Our truest form of living is in following His words. The highest form of devotion; to submit to His call. Other pursuits may appeal for a time, but our Savior's call lasts eternally. Let us look to none other than our Lord. He holds the words of eternal life.

Share your experience now at
www.ThirstNoMoreBook.com.

SEPTEMBER 30

"My time is not yet here."
—John 7:6

As the Festival of Tabernacles approached, Christ's brothers encouraged Him to go to Judea. Why? To increase His popularity. To their deceitful scheme, Jesus replied, "My time is not yet here; for you any time will do." Their lack of conviction highlighted His utmost convictions. His time would come, but according to the Father's plan, not human plans.

In our desire to prove ourselves, any time can be claimed as "the right time." But God's pace and ours often conflict; He desires to bring Himself glory; we often seek our own. Let us not live with regret at opportunities missed, but with respect toward Christ's opportunities. We need not rush our spiritual journey; let us savor each moment of the walk with our Savior.

Share your experience now at
www.ThirstNoMoreBook.com.

"Stop judging by mere appearances."
—John 7:24

To judge, we tend to declare someone right and another person wrong. Jesus did not condemn judgment by His opponents; only that they judge accurately. They had judged Him because He had healed someone on the Sabbath. In doing so, they missed the purpose of Christ's healing—to reveal the coming of God's Messiah.

It is much easier to condemn another than see the larger picture. God is often up to something our eyes miss because of our criticisms of others. Rather than jump to a conclusion about the decisions of others, we do well to reflect on our own faults and how we can help others in their journey. There may be a time for correction, but let it begin in our own hearts first.

Share your experience now at
www.ThirstNoMoreBook.com.

OCTOBER 2

"Let anyone who is thirsty come."
—John 7:37

Jesus quenches thirst. He compels the thirsty to come to Him: "Let anyone who is thirsty come to me and drink." This call includes a variety of parts. First, Jesus calls "anyone." All are invited. Second, He invites the "thirsty." Those willing to come must have a craving to motivate their coming.

Third, the command is to "come." Christ does not send us away, but bids us to join to Him in His presence. Finally, we "drink." He gives living water, for He is the Water of life. We who thirst can only be quenched in Him. No other drink, no other pursuit, satisfies permanently. He is our Water. In Him, we will thirst no more: "Let anyone who is thirsty come."

Share your experience now at
www.ThirstNoMoreBook.com.

OCTOBER 3

"I am the light of the world."
—John 8:12

Light and dark. Neither can exist in the presence of the other. Jesus called Himself the Light of the world, referring to His power over spiritual darkness. He had the audacity to proclaim, "Whoever follows me will never walk in darkness." In Him, we not only find light; we escape darkness completely.

This glorious truth does not indicate we will never falter in our walk with Christ; it means in Him we have power over the darkness. Satan and his forces of evil are strong, but no match to the Spirit of God living in us through Christ. His power that created the mountains, the land, the sea, and everything in the sea lives within us. He is the Light of the world.

Share your experience now at
www.ThirstNoMoreBook.com.

October 4

"The truth will set you free."
—John 8:32

Deceit imprisons. In contrast, truth sets us free. Jesus made clear to those who had believed in Him, "If you hold to my teaching, you are really my disciples. Then you will know the truth, and the truth will set you free." True followers stay focused. Real focus gives freedom.

The call of Christ is rarely convenient. He demands our full devotion, in good times and bad. Yet in following Him, we know truth; in knowing truth, we know freedom. Freedom is the source of true life, regarding of the difficulties we may face. May He find us among those who hold to His teaching; may we experience true freedom as followers of the One True King: "The truth will set you free."

Share your experience now at
www.ThirstNoMoreBook.com.

OCTOBER 5

"Everyone who sins is a slave to sin."
—John 8:34

Our sins make us slaves. We frequently seek to look good by comparing our weaknesses to someone in a worse situation. Jesus made clear, "Everyone who sins is a slave to sin." A slave has no status as family. Due to sin, we are separated from the family of God.

This demeaning state contrasts with our eternal freedom in Christ. In Him, we are no longer slaves. Rather, we are children of the King. In a culture where the status between slave and son stood in stark contrast, Christ's words poked deep into the emotions of the human condition. In our lives, we innately despise the evil oppression of slavery. The difference between bondage and freedom is Jesus. Let us cherish our role as His children.

Share your experience now at
www.ThirstNoMoreBook.com.

"If the Son sets you free, you will be free indeed."
—John 8:36

In ancient culture, freed slaves often became slaves again to other masters. Without family or financial status, the cycle often repeated itself within different households. Freedom was not always freedom. Jesus picked up on this cultural phenomenon to point to the perfect freedom He offers: "If the Son sets you free, you will be free indeed."

Freedom is not truly freedom unless our freedom endures. To be "free indeed" indicates a lasting opportunity for new life. In Christ, this new life extends throughout eternity. We live comforted in the news that eternity is not another location to repeat the injustices of this world, but rather to celebrate the perfect justice of our heavenly Father. Let us walk in His freedom today.

Share your experience now at
www.ThirstNoMoreBook.com.

"I have come here from God."
—John 8:42

Jesus exchanged heaven for earth. He dwelt in perfection; He entered imperfection. Why? God sent Him: "I have come here from God. I have not come on my own; God sent me." As One sent from God, His message held authority, yet His opponents criticized His words and His works.

As we shake our heads at Christ's critics, we need only look to ourselves to find a modern example of similar treatment. Our Lord speaks truth; yet we find ourselves seeking shortcuts to following His call. Our Lord gives wisdom, yet we neglect it for our own conveniences. Jesus came from eternity to earth to speak wisdom for our lives. Let us not view His commands as anything but perfect words from a loving God.

Share your experience now at
www.ThirstNoMoreBook.com.

"Whoever belongs to God hears what God says."
—John 8:47

Hearing is more than noting the sounds coming from another object or person. In Scripture, hearing often includes the idea of hearing with the desire to apply what has been spoken. With this understanding, Christ's words take on a deeper meaning: "Whoever belongs to God hears what God says."

We do more than understand His words; we seek to obey them. Any listener can comprehend what Christ speaks; only a follower will truly "hear" them. We belong to God, therefore we seek to live His words as our will. He has spoken; we need only comprehend and commit to application. Let us hear from the Savior, let us heed His sayings. His words are words of life. Let us make them our way of life.

Share your experience now at
www.ThirstNoMoreBook.com.

"Before Abraham was born, I am!"
—John 8:58

Christ is eternal God. Though called God's Son, the Father did not give birth to Him. He has existed with the Father and Spirit throughout eternity in perfect community and love. This is why He could say, "Before Abraham was born, I am!"

The name "I am" refers to God's encounter with Moses at the burning bush. "I am" was the name God revealed for Himself. Christ was present at the bush, before Abraham, and even before creation. We have been on His mind since before the stars, moon, and sun were hung. He has intimately designed us for His purposes. We are unique and loved in Him. Let us live with confidence in our Creator today; let us live His purposes this day.

Share your experience now at
www.ThirstNoMoreBook.com.

"That the works of God might be displayed."
—John 9:3

On one occasion, the disciples asked Jesus about a man who had been born blind: "Who sinned, this man or his parents, that he was born blind?" Their question betrayed the attitude of a culture that saw disability as God's judgment. But Jesus quickly corrected their thinking. This man's blindness was not a judgment of God, but an opportunity for God.

Jesus placed mud and saliva on the man's eyes, instructing him to wash in the Pool of Siloam. When he did, he could see! God can use weakness for His glory. He desires to use our weaknesses, too. Let us stand before Christ, following His instructions for cleansing and spiritual sight. Let us seek that God's work might be displayed in our lives.

Share your experience now at
www.ThirstNoMoreBook.com.

OCTOBER 11

"I am the light of the world."
—John 9:5

Light provides sight. Jesus restored the eyes of the blind. He alone could claim, "I am the light of the world." Light offers heat and direction in times of cold and darkness. Likewise, Jesus is our warmth, our guide. Apart from Him, we would stumble and fall. With Him, we find our way through the dark void of life.

There is one additional aspect of light—energy. Light is a source, just as Jesus is our source of life. The light of fire must originate from some spark; our Light is both the spark and the fire. He is the Light of the world; we need only come to Him to find our way; we need only depend on His guidance for our journey.

Share your experience now at
www.ThirstNoMoreBook.com.

OCTOBER 12

"I was blind but now I see."
—John 9:25

A man born blind could now see. People rejoiced, yet the Pharisees called this man's story into question. They brought the man into their presence for questioning. He could not answer all of their accusations, but the healed man did have one answer. "One thing I know. I was blind but now I see."

We often struggle to answer those who question our faith. In our insecurity, we find it easier not to speak at all. But this man provides a different alternative. Rather than argue with those who inquired, he answered with the one thing he did know with certainty. His life had been radically changed. His life was his answer. Let our lives be the answer to the questions of others.

Share your experience now at
www.ThirstNoMoreBook.com.

"Lord, I believe."
—John 9:38

Belief involves understanding and faith. When Jesus appeared to the blind man He had healed, He asked, "Do you believe in the Son of Man?" The man did not believe because he did not know who the Son of Man was.

The healed man asked, "Who is he? Tell me so that I may believe in him." Jesus revealed Himself as Son of Man: "You have now seen him." The man immediately believed. To believe, we need to know who to believe and then do so in faith. Our faith need not be blind, but informed. Let us seek to know our Lord deeply; let believe more deeply, too. Let the result of our learning always be, "Lord, I believe."

Share your experience now at
www.ThirstNoMoreBook.com.

"They know his voice."
—John 10:4

Sheep follow the voice of their shepherd. When the voice of another resounds, the sheep do not respond. Only the shepherd's words find meaning in their ears. Comfort, nourishment, and protection are all found in the sound of the shepherd's voice.

When Jesus speaks, do we hear Him as our shepherd? Too often, we see ourselves as the shepherds. At other times, we obey as sheep but find the voice of others tempting us away from our true Shepherd. But His sheep know His voice. We are not the shepherd, nor do we follow the noise of others. Our only hope lies in obedience to the One who leads us. In His voice, we find our needs met. In Him, we have complete satisfaction.

Share your experience now at
www.ThirstNoMoreBook.com.

"I am the gate for the sheep."
—John 10:7

Christ is not only the shepherd; He is also the sheep gate. No one can enter without passing through Him. All who enter through Him are saved; they are satisfied. Sheep cannot last for long without protection. Left to their own strength, robbers or predators soon arrive to attack. Only with a shepherd can sheep find protection. Only by entering the gate can they find a place of refuge.

These words of our Lord reveal two purposes. First, He is the only source of salvation. None other can provide for our souls. Second, He protects us from the enemies of our souls. He saves us and secures us. We can walk safely in Him today. He is the gate for the sheep.

Share your experience now at
www.ThirstNoMoreBook.com.

"That they may have life."
—John 10:10

Our spiritual enemy desires to take life; our Lord desires give life. This life is not mere existence, but life at its fullest potential. "I have come that they may have life, and have it to the full." Many see Jesus as a ticket to heaven, but such a perspective misses His intent. "To the full" does not necessarily mean more in this world, but a daily joy that our souls experience through the very presence of Christ.

If we could keep our eyes on the eternity that awaits us, our daily routine would include infinitely more joy. Eternal life actually starts the moment we begin our journey in Christ; let us live mindful of this truth throughout every moment of the day.

Share your experience now at
www.ThirstNoMoreBook.com.

"I am the good shepherd."
—John 10:14

A good shepherd knows his sheep; his sheep know him. In fact, a good shepherd is willing to give his life on behalf of his sheep to protect them from harm. Jesus used this analogy of Himself: "I am the good shepherd." He knows us. We know Him. He has given His life for us.

Another deep connection between the good shepherd and his sheep is that they dwell together. A shepherd could not care for his sheep without being there day and night. Likewise, our Lord knows us and is there for us in our time of need. Let us not live as if we can hide from Him; let us treasure that He hears us every moment. He is our Good Shepherd.

Share your experience now at
www.ThirstNoMoreBook.com.

"I and the Father are one."
—John 10:30

To claim equality with God was the highest crime in Jewish culture. When Jesus spoke these words, His opponents picked up stones to kill Him. Still today, many view Jesus as an influential teacher or leader, but will not accept Him as God. How are Jesus and the Father one?

The early church fathers struggled to put words to this equation. How can Jesus be one with the Father. In human terms, they taught Jesus is one in essence with the Father as the second person of the Triune God. Jesus is God, making Him one with God the Father and God the Spirit. The Creator of us all came to die for us all. Let us see Him not simply as leader, but as Lord.

Share your experience now at
www.ThirstNoMoreBook.com.

OCTOBER 19

"It is for God's glory."
—John 11:4

Have you ever wondered why God allows us to be sick? Couldn't we serve Him more effectively healthy? Yet Jesus notes one occasion in which sickness was for God's glory. The disciples could not understand His actions. Why not heal Lazarus now? Didn't He care about His friend's illness?

But Jesus had another plan. His plan included using sickness and even death to bring God honor. Do not question God's motives; seek God's glory. Don't doubt God's heart; desire God's honor. He has made clear His love for us. He cares about us more than we care about ourselves. The pain He allows is not without purpose. When we struggle, it is for our Savior. "It is for God's glory."

Share your experience now at
www.ThirstNoMoreBook.com.

"I am the resurrection and the life."
—John 11:25

Jesus can resurrect life because He created life. In the case of Lazarus, He restored His friend to life to prove His power over death. Shortly afterwards, Jesus would even allow His own death. He would likewise follow with resurrection from the dead.

When we believe in Christ as the Messiah, He lives within us. The same resurrection power that returned Lazarus to life and later Jesus Himself beats within our hearts. No problem in this world can conquer us. No weapon of the enemy can destroy us. Christ's power is limitless; when He lives in us, all things become possible for us as well. Jesus is the resurrection and the life. Let us walk knowing His power is within us today.

Share your experience now at
www.ThirstNoMoreBook.com.

OCTOBER 21

"Jesus wept."
—John 11:35

The shortest verse in Scripture is one of the most powerful. When Jesus stood before the tomb of His friend Lazarus, "Jesus wept." To weep indicates more than a few tears; rather, He responded to the death of this man as if He had lost a close family member. Those nearby reacted, saying, "See how he loved him!" His tears revealed His love.

Christ cares for us with the same love. This love that caused our Lord to weep at the tomb of Lazarus would soon hold Him to the Cross to redeem us. His same compassion would be expressed through the nails in His feet and hands. His love transcends our understanding, but we must understand He loves us deeply.

Share your experience now at
www.ThirstNoMoreBook.com.

"We would like to see Jesus."
—John 12:21

The religious leaders sought to kill Jesus; seekers sought to see Jesus. Some of the Greeks who had traveled to Jerusalem for the Passover desired to meet with the One many were calling the Messiah. But how would they find Him? These men found Jesus through His followers. Philip and Andrew were the men responsible for connecting these inquirers with Christ.

Many continue to seek Christ; their problem is finding Him. God has chosen us as those who can connect others to Him. We know the way to the Master; part of our work is to connect others to Him. He does the conversion, we do the connection. Let us pray and pursue bringing others who say, "We would like to see Jesus."

Share your experience now at
www.ThirstNoMoreBook.com.

"Where I am, my servant also will be."
—John 12:26

Servants serve masters. Masters lead homes. To know to whom a servant belongs, we need only to look to their master. The master's home is the servant's home. If we belong to Christ, we know our home is with Him forever. But entry to this kingdom requires something—service.

Serving a master is not optional; it is a given. Only when we view our relationship with Christ as a worker required to perform the wishes of the Master do we see our place clearly. Unlike some earthly masters, our Master will honor us in the kingdom. How? By granting us eternity in His presence. There are also rewards for service. How will we show we are His servants today? Let us do so through a life that reflects His attitude and His actions.

Share your experience now at
www.ThirstNoMoreBook.com.

"He loved them to the end."
—John 13:1

Human love is limited. Friends move apart, relationships break up, families live in conflict. Perhaps this is why the love of Jesus is so striking. Christ's love is unlimited. One aspect of this supernatural love is found in the words, "He loved them to the end." His followers would include a betrayer, a denier, and ten others who would flee at His time of greatest need. Yet He would love them until His last dying breath...and beyond.

We struggle to show compassion to those who care for us; we find it impossible to care for those who mistreat us. Only through Christ is such unconditional love possible. We can love despite circumstances because He loves us despite our circumstances. Let us "love to the end" today.

Share your experience now at
www.ThirstNoMoreBook.com.

"He...began to wash his disciples' feet."
—John 13:5

Love drove Jesus to His knees. On His last night with His followers, He chose to lower Himself by washing their feet. This action was the work of a lowly servant; not one of the Twelve had chosen to initiate the effort. Rather than enjoy a meal relaxed, they chose to sit with dirty feet.

This condition provided Jesus an opportunity to express His love in a powerful way. He had spoken to His followers of His love; now He showed it through practical action. This day, we will find a situation in need of our love in action. Let us follow the example of our Lord. Let us speak love—and show it. Let us wash the "dirty feet" we encounter in our journey.

Share your experience now at
www.ThirstNoMoreBook.com.

October 26

"Do you understand what I have done?"
—John 13:12

Jesus washed feet for a reason. He first asked His followers if they understood His purpose: "Do you understand what I have done for you?" They did not. Peter had initially refused. The other Eleven remained speechless. Why would their Master take on the task of the lowest servant?

His purpose was to provide an example. It is one thing to teach well; it is another to live well. Jesus had taught them many truths in their time together; tonight He had lived truth in their presence. Christ provided the perfect example in all things—His teachings, His cross, and the menial task of cleaning toes. Let us follow His example in all areas of life, even if our journey leads to washing feet.

Share your experience now at
www.ThirstNoMoreBook.com.

"Blessed if you do them."
—John 13:17

Learning builds our lives, serving blesses them. After Jesus washed the feet of His followers, He taught, "Now that you know these things, you will be blessed if you do them." Blessing follows action. Without application of truth, we fail to receive the blessing our Lord desires to provide. Both are essential.

Jesus stayed with His followers for three years to prepare them for a lifetime of service. His mentoring prepared the way for their mission. They would know their role as servants and be ready to serve, following the example of their Master. Let us, too, focus on God's truth that we may be God's truth to someone today. Let us receive the blessing that comes from doing the works of our Lord.

Share your experience now at
www.ThirstNoMoreBook.com.

"The Son of Man is glorified."
—John 13:31

Jesus was consumed with bringing glory to God. On the night of His betrayal, He claimed, "Now the Son of Man is glorified and God is glorified in him. If God is glorified in him, God will glorify the Son in himself, and will glorify him at once." Five times Jesus speaks of glory. He repeatedly referred to glory as His ultimate desire.

Christ desires us to be about His glory as well. Our understanding, our thoughts, our actions—all are to bring glory to Him. Our standard must not be to live more holy than the person next to us; our standard must be His standard, His honor, His glory. Let us be consumed by what brings Him glory today.

Share your experience now at
www.ThirstNoMoreBook.com.

"Love one another."
—John 13:34

Christ's final night before His death included a new command to His friends: "Love one another." They were to love each other as Christ had loved them. They were not only to follow His example in service; they were to follow His example in love. When Jesus spoke these words, His followers would have gulped at the implications. He had called them, taught them, forgiven them, all with no strings attached. He was now calling them to do the same for one another.

One of our most powerful influences in the lives of others is how we treat those in the family of God. Likewise, one of the most negative influences is when we treat one another poorly. Let us love one another.

Share your experience now at
www.ThirstNoMoreBook.com.

OCTOBER 30

"By this everyone will know."
—John 13:35

How do people recognize that we follow Jesus? One clear way is the love we have for one another. When we love across all lines of race, economics, social class, and nationality, we reflect something from beyond this world. Our planet contains a myriad of examples of groups who love those within their tribe and exclude those outside of it. Those who love one another as Christ loves defy this pattern.

When we no longer fit the norms of our society, our society notices. When they see a deep, unconditional love, they note we are following the way of Jesus. Perhaps this is why our Lord left us the words, "By this everyone will know that you are my disciples, if you love one another."

Share your experience now at
www.ThirstNoMoreBook.com.

"Do not let your hearts be troubled."
—John 14:1

Before Jesus left, He told His followers not to let their hearts be troubled. Why? He offered multiple reasons. First, because of Christ Himself: "You believe in God; believe also in me." Second, because of heaven: "My Father's house has many rooms." Third, because He will return: "If I go and prepare a place for you, I will come back and take you to be with me."

Christ. Heaven. Christ's return. These three foundations serve as our hope when the temptation is for our hearts to be troubled. Christ is there, heaven is coming, and Christ will soon return to take His own to be with Him forever. When we remind ourselves of these promises, our hearts can survive, and even thrive, under any circumstances.

Share your experience now at
www.ThirstNoMoreBook.com.

November 1

"My Father's house has many rooms."
—John 14:2

In the ancient world of Jesus, a family's home often included extensions to include new children and extended family. Jesus used this image to speak of our heavenly Father's home. In His house, there are many rooms. We need not worry if there is enough space for us all. Christ has personally returned to heaven to prepare a place for all of His people.

Another promise in these words is Christ's return. He did not leave for long; He will soon come back to take us, His family, to our heavenly home. We may not know where it is, but we know the Way who will take us there. Our "Father's house has many rooms." He has a special place for each of us.

Share your experience now at
www.ThirstNoMoreBook.com.

"I am the way and the truth and the life."
—John 14:6

When we thirst, there is only one answer—a drink. The same is true for our souls. Our souls thirst. There is only one drink that will quench its longing—Jesus. He clearly expressed He is the way, the truth, the life.

Other spiritual systems may satisfy in part or for a time, but leave our souls longing for more. This is because Jesus is the only drink—the only source—that eternally satisfies. All other options simply offer a way. Jesus is the way. Many believe such teaching is outdated or even arrogant. But if it's true, then our greatest response is to embrace Christ, live His truth, and share His life with others. "I am the way and the truth and the life."

Share your experience now at
www.ThirstNoMoreBook.com.

NOVEMBER 3

"If you love me, keep my commands."
—John 14:15

As children, our parents expected certain actions from us. We often did not understand it at the time, but later realized these instructions were based on their love for us. Jesus is the same in this regard. Rather than viewing His commands as harsh limitations on our human freedoms, we are to see them as teachings based on His great love for us.

Likewise, we show our love to Him through keeping His commands. Prayer, service to the poor, or other noble pursuits are not to prove our commitment to Him, but to express our love for Him. We love Him not only through songs and intercessions, but by keeping His commands. For those who love Christ, obedience is not based on duty but devotion.

Share your experience now at
www.ThirstNoMoreBook.com.

NOVEMBER 4

"He will give you another advocate."
—John 14:16

Jesus promised His followers another advocate or lawyer-counselor. Who is it? The Holy Spirit. The Spirit will "be with us forever." How does the Spirit help? God's Spirit lives within us, His own, forever. Jesus came to earth for a brief time. The Spirit comes into us for all time. What Jesus revealed in His life lives within our lives through the Holy Spirit of God.

Many have feared the Holy Spirit through the years. The Spirit has even been called a "ghost" by older translations But Jesus made clear the Spirit is our advocate. He works on our behalf as "another advocate" similar to Jesus. He is perfect and powerful enough to strengthen us for the calling of God today.

Share your experience now at
www.ThirstNoMoreBook.com.

NOVEMBER 5

"The Spirit of truth."
—John 14:17

The Holy Spirit is the Spirit of truth. He will never lead us into error. God's Spirit points to the works of the Son and the power of the Father. He can do nothing but reflect the glory of the perfect Triune God.

We frequently question whether an impulse is from God's Spirit or our human desires. How can we know the difference? One way is to compare our desire to what God has revealed in Scripture. The Spirit will never lead us to actions contrary to God's declared truth. He will lead us to convictions that increase the glory of the Father and not our own. Only then can we consider a conviction within us to be from God's Spirit.

Share your experience now at
www.ThirstNoMoreBook.com.

"I will not leave you as orphans."
—John 14:18

Orphans are vulnerable. The reason we place priority to helping orphans is because they cannot help themselves. They are without father or mother to provide for their needs. Christ made clear this is not His plan for His followers: "I will not leave you as orphans."

Instead, Jesus promised to return. He returned from death and ascended to heaven. He will also return again, taking us to be with Him forever. We are not alone. He is with us. We can walk securely, for our Lord lives. We can walk in confidence, for He has promised to return. We can walk in joy, for our Father loves us. He will not leave us as orphans. We belong to the family of God.

Share your experience now at
www.ThirstNoMoreBook.com.

November 7

"The one who loves me."
—John 14:21

How do we know a person loves Jesus? "Whoever has my commands and keeps them is the one who loves me." He has made clear that the love of Christ is revealed through our obedience to Christ. Many claim the name Christian; few live like Christ. The only clear way to know if we belong to Him is if our lives reflect His. In this way, we remove all doubt that He lives within us.

Our salvation is by faith alone in Christ; our lives are to reflect this faith. When we do, others see Jesus in us. His message spreads, His love flourishes. May we be among those who reveal the life of our Master; may we those who love Him by keeping His commands.

Share your experience now at
www.ThirstNoMoreBook.com.

"Anyone who loves me."
—John 14:23

Jesus gave one stipulation for all who love Him: "Anyone who loves me will obey my teaching." Love is shown through our lives. The first step is to learn His teachings. We must know truth to live it. As we meditate upon Scripture, we discover His principles. As we consider His ways, we change our ways.

The second step is to obey truth. We can know much, yet live little. We can study diligently, yet live hesitantly. Our desire must be to know much and to love much. This combination is Christ's ideal. Let us commit ourselves anew to His words; let us conform ourselves afresh to His ways. May the One within us be seen among those who meet us this day.

Share your experience now at
www.ThirstNoMoreBook.com.

"The Holy Spirit ... will remind you."
—John 14:26

The Holy Spirit reminds us of God's holiness. He not only teaches, but refreshes our memory. When we stray, He strengthens. There are moments in life when we forget our first love. The pleasure of the moment appeals at the time of temptation. In our weakness, the Spirit works best.

His reminding leads to our remembering. In remembering, the voice of Christ becomes clear once again in our time of struggle. He rescues from the consequences of sin that would have otherwise been committed. In conviction, we find Christ's teachings. In His teachings, we find our way, a way greater than the things of this world, but rather eternal. He will remind us of Jesus, the One who redeemed us.

Share your experience now at
www.ThirstNoMoreBook.com.

"Peace I leave with you."
—John 14:27

Many proclaim their longing for world peace, but Jesus has already provided peace for His followers. Peace is not something reserved for the future; peace is here and now.

Jesus said He does not give as the world gives. By that, He expressed His eternal peace, something that cannot be won through wars or lost through earthly demise. God's peace comes from Himself within the Christian. Those of us who have experienced God's peace are called to share it with others. Despite external circumstances, we can point the way to a peace that is beyond this world, lasting for eternity. The tranquility of the soul provides a hope for now and the future. Christ's peace removes fear; Christ's peace provides hope. "Peace I leave with you."

Share your experience now at
www.ThirstNoMoreBook.com.

"I am the true vine."
—John 15:1

Jesus often used illustrations from the world of agriculture. One of His most powerful was the account of Jesus as the "true vine." Our Christ distinguished Himself as One who was real, distinct from all other vines.

Most importantly, Jesus revealed that we must be connected to this True Vine. Apart from this Vine, we die. Apart from Him, we have no life. The daily temptation is to live as if we are the vine and Jesus is the branch. We see ourselves as the primary force and Him as one aspect of life. Yet our only true response is full dependence on our True Vine. Apart from Him and His grace we can do nothing. "I am the true vine."

Share your experience now at
www.ThirstNoMoreBook.com.

"He prunes."
—John 15:2

What did Jesus mean when He taught, "Every branch that does bear fruit he prunes so that it will be even more fruitful"? A pruned branch is a cut branch. A pruned branch is trimmed back to move forward stronger. This is His intention for us.

Our grief is for growth. Our struggle is intended to strengthen. Just as a pruned branch can result in increased fruit, so our pruning can result in greater fruit for God's garden. Though painful, our utmost desire must be the pleasure of our Gardener, the Father. Seen through His eyes, we can know our growth is His goal; our greater abundance is His glory. Let us endure God's pruning as His favor, a favor that leads to further growth.

Share your experience now at
www.ThirstNoMoreBook.com.

"Apart from me you can do nothing."
—John 15:5

Jesus makes clear our complete dependence upon Him. In Him, we can bear much fruit. Without Him, we will be fruitless: "Apart from me you can do nothing." Just as a branch cut from a vine has no life, so we have no life without remaining connected to the vine of Christ.

We often speak confidently of our human abilities, claiming, "We can do it!" Such encouragement apart from Christ is senseless. Self-empowerment apart from surrender to Jesus is fruitless. With Him, all things are possible; apart from Him the opposite is true. Without Him, we are branches good for nothing but fire. Our only hope can be found in the mercies of our Lord. Let us stay connected to the Vine.

Share your experience now at
www.ThirstNoMoreBook.com.

"Now remain in my love."
—John 15:9

What does it mean to remain in Christ's love? Jesus explains it is to keep His commands, just as He kept the Father's commands. How did Christ keep the Father's commands? Completely. He did not hold back or give halfhearted effort. He patiently followed His plan from birth to death to resurrection.

Our lives must reflect Christ's obedience to the Father. He calls us to follow without holding back, giving full attention to His will. When we do, we remain in His love. We experience the best He has for our lives. We enjoy the same love that exists between the Son and the Father. Our intimacy with Christ will exist at its highest when we shine His holiness. Let us remain in His love.

Share your experience now at
www.ThirstNoMoreBook.com.

"Love each other as I have loved you."
—John 15:12

Example. We learn by viewing; we live by doing. The night before Jesus suffered on the Cross, He left the command to love each other as He had loved them. He did not tell His disciples to live out what they had read or to live merely by His teachings. Jesus led by His lifestyle.

Likewise, someone will be watching our lives today. Will we be able to say, as Jesus did, "Love each other as I have loved you"? This is a convicting, challenging goal. To live like Christ means to love like Christ. Only through modeling our life after His will we influence those around us at the deepest level. He is our standard. We must love as He has loved us.

Share your experience now at
www.ThirstNoMoreBook.com.

"I have called you friends."
—John 15:15

The differences between a friend and servant are vast. A servant is compelled to work for another; a friend chooses to care for the other. Servants assume a lesser role; friends share an equal role. When Jesus called His followers "friends," He conferred a level of intimacy not traditionally associated with God. Ancient people thought of deity as far-removed; Christ brushed elbows with His "friends."

Further, servants are often only given enough information to perform their task. Jesus also called His disciples friends because He had revealed to them "everything that I learned from my Father." They would end that night saddened at Christ's outcome, not only because they had lost their Master, but because they had lost their friend. We are friends of God.

Share your experience now at
www.ThirstNoMoreBook.com.

"I chose you."
—John 15:16

We do not choose Christ; He chooses us: "I chose you." Choice implies consideration, contemplation, selection. Jesus carefully decided before the foundations of the earth to choose you as His child. In doing so, there is a profound realization that when we came to Christ in our brokenness, He has already prepared the way. Further, He placed the desire within us to seek and to find Him.

In His vast love, no detail was excluded from His process. Our family heritage, our birthplace, our parents—everything! Every aspect of our lives reflects a portion of His plan to pursue and choose us. Why? Ultimately, because of His love, a love we may not understand but willingly accept. In His love, He chose us.

Share your experience now at
www.ThirstNoMoreBook.com.

"Fruit that will last."
—John 15:16

What is fruit that lasts? Christ chooses us to bear fruit that will last, but we often neglect to consider the influence He has granted. Fruit that lasts speaks of actions that alter matters for eternity. Lasting fruit makes a difference both now and forever. We were made to make a difference.

We are transformed to transform. We, as His fruit, bear fruit that again multiplies through successive generations of life. Our opportunities extend well past our lives, but toward an enduring legacy of lives impacted by our interactions today. Each word and action we share touches the next century. Let us not be discouraged by the weight of this responsibility. Rather, let us walk wisely that we may better produce "fruit that will last."

Share your experience now at
www.ThirstNoMoreBook.com.

"The prince of this world now stands condemned."
—John 16:11

Satan has been defeated. Through Christ, Satan stands condemned. His power may last for a moment, but His judgment will stand for eternity. As we embrace Christ, Satan's power in our lives becomes defeated. He may continue to tempt, but we now have Christ's power to resist.

In the wilderness, Jesus revealed the way to handle the devil's schemes. When we quote God's truth, we shield ourselves from Satan's attacks. Satan soon flees, waiting to return later for another battle. In our human frailty, we will at times succumb to his tactics. However, we are no longer under Satan's power or control. No weapon formed against us will prosper. We belong to Christ. "The prince of this world now stands condemned."

Share your experience now at
www.ThirstNoMoreBook.com.

"Your joy will be complete."
—John 16:24

What did Jesus call the completion of our joy? Receiving the answer to our prayers. Answered prayers are more than a dream come true; they are conversations with God coming to completion. Jesus calls us to ask for anything in His name and we will receive. This does not promise a blank check, but rather a commitment Christ will follow through when we pray in alignment with His desires.

To many, praying "in Jesus' name" is nothing more than saying "the end" to conclude a prayer. But the implication is much deeper. Previously, God's people had been required to offer a sacrifice, come to the temple, or stand before a priest. These traditions would no longer be necessary. All that is necessary is Christ. He provides complete joy.

Share your experience now at
www.ThirstNoMoreBook.com.

"I am not alone, for my Father is with me."
—John 16:32

Have you ever felt alone? We all have. But Jesus shares a brief insight that shatters our perspective of loneliness. He predicted before His arrest that all would leave Him. Yet He also taught He would not be alone because His Father would be with Him.

You are never alone. You can talk with Him and trust that He hears you at all times. He is never too busy, nor too far away, nor too tired to listen. In fact, He longs for us to spend time in His presence. Jesus modeled what it means to live alone without being alone. Relationships with others are critical, but even if all others fail you, God is there. He is listening. He is with you.

Share your experience now at
www.ThirstNoMoreBook.com.

"Now this is eternal life."
—John 17:3

We tend to see eternal life as a celestial party. God is there, our friends and family, and some angels. But this is an inaccurate picture of what "eternal life" means. Jesus made it clear: "Now this is eternal life: that they know you, the only true God, and Jesus Christ." Eternal life is knowing God.

One amazing insight from this definition is that eternal life has already begun! If we know God, our eternity is in progress. We don't simply look forward to eternal life—we're living it! Heaven lies ahead in our future, but our eternal life began with knowing God through His Son and continues even now. We are living eternal life. Let us shine His eternal life to others this day.

Share your experience now at
www.ThirstNoMoreBook.com.

"That they may be one as we are one."
—John 17:11

Christ prayed for the unity of His followers. In fact, He prayed for them to "be one as we are one." His desire was that the community among His followers achieves something similar to the relationship between Father and Son. This profound request strikes against the individualism of our time. In an age of celebrities and heroes, Jesus calls us to seek the type of unity as revealed in the perfect community between Father and Son.

Forsaking all to follow Christ does not mean to forsake all people. We are called to live in harmony with our brothers and sisters, reflecting a oneness unknown to this world. As we do, we reflect God's glory and stand as witness of our Master's love.

Share your experience now at
www.ThirstNoMoreBook.com.

"They are not of the world."
—John 17:16

As Christ's followers, we are not "of the world." We are no longer owned by its system or its values. In Christ, we are a new creation. This truth highlights we are in the world but not of it. We walk the earth, yet are no longer its citizens. Our kingdom is from above, in the heavens. We are simply passing through this life.

This eternal viewpoint should impact our lives now. Our attachment to worldly possessions will be light; our human pursuits in light of God's glory. When we see life from the perspective of our heavenly home, our earthly home becomes but a temporary respite in pursuit of our ultimate resting place—in His presence. Let us live mindful of our heavenly dwelling today.

Share your experience now at
www.ThirstNoMoreBook.com.

"Your word is truth."
—John 17:17

God's Word is truth. Christ declared this; Scripture affirms it. The holy text is not simple historical literature or inspired in part; it is a very extension of God Himself. When we hear it we hear God; when we read it we sense God.

Scripture opens our eyes to God's view of life and eternity. No longer must we stumble through life, guessing His will or perspective regarding our challenges. His truth makes clear His thoughts on many matters. His attributes, His works, and His glory all receive attention in its pages. As His children, we must seek to know, to understand, to live. The Word is worthy of our work. Scripture's divine nature demands our sacred devotion: "Your word is truth."

Share your experience now at
www.ThirstNoMoreBook.com.

"I have sent them into the world."
—John 17:18

We are set apart to serve. Our Lord was sent into the world to send others. We, too, fall into this line of saints who serve. Whether near or far, in high or low places, we each have a call from God to make a difference in the lives of others. To neglect this call is to miss our true calling; to embrace it, our highest calling.

To serve, we must submit. When we submit to our Master, we begin to see Jesus in the eyes of those we encounter each day. As we show honor to them, we show honor to Him. As we give respect to our neighbor, we show respect to our Savior. We are saved to be sent.

Share your experience now at
www.ThirstNoMoreBook.com.

"I pray also for those who will believe."
—John 17:20

Christ prayed for us during His last night on earth. This humbling thought sweeps through the pages of history to where we stand at this moment. What did Jesus pray for us? "That all of them may be one." His singular request He made on our behalf was for unity.

Why unity? That the world may believe Christ has sent us. Our divisions cast doubt to the unbelieving world that our message is from beyond this world. When others see a difference in our relationships, they often desire to meet the Reason behind our community. Let us live united with our brothers and sisters in the faith. We will then answer the prayer of Christ and draw more to His name.

Share your experience now at
www.ThirstNoMoreBook.com.

*"Shall I not drink the cup
the Father has given me?"*
—John 18:11

When something goes wrong, it is easy to blame God. But problems are sometimes from God for a purpose. When Jesus was arrested, the Apostle Peter cut the ear off of Malchus. Jesus stopped him and healed the man, asking, "Shall I not drink the cup the Father has given me?"

His response stands as our pattern. When pain arrives, we desire to cut it off immediately. But perhaps God would have us to endure for a purpose greater than the pain itself. This does not belittle our pain or problems, but does mean they serve a purpose. If Christ's death on the Cross can be part of God's will, couldn't we view our daily frustrations with a similar perspective?

Share your experience now at
www.ThirstNoMoreBook.com.

"Ask those who heard me."
—John 18:21

When Jesus was questioned during His trial about His disciples and teaching, He replied, "Ask those who heard me." Why? Because the true test of a person's life and teachings comes from the lives impacted. The people are the proof.

This convicting observation applies to our lives today. If someone asks those closest to us about our life and teachings, what would they hear? If you are concerned with what the response might be, the good news is that there is still time to change. Live in such a way today that those closest to you would clearly know the Christ you follow and what you believe. Live so that you may someday confidently suggest, "Ask those who heard me."

Share your experience now at
www.ThirstNoMoreBook.com.

"Didn't I see you with him?"
—John 18:26

Peter faced the question a third time: "Didn't I see you with him in the garden? A third time he denied knowing Christ. A rooster crowed. Christ's prediction had come to pass.

The most prominent follower of Jesus turned on Him at His most critical moment. Peter, however, was later restored to service. Why? God's forgiveness. We tend to believe our mistakes end our ministry; our temporary flaws turn us into lasting failures. Despite our weaknesses, He continues to forgive. Even more, He continues to use us for His glory. What a wonderful Lord! No other provides such understanding and restoration. Regardless of our failures, let us embrace His forgiveness. Let us press on to live out His forgiveness in our lives.

Share your experience now at
www.ThirstNoMoreBook.com.

December 1

"My kingdom is not of this world."
—John 18:36

The busyness of life often tempts us to believe this world is all there is. The next project, the next meeting, the next big thing. But Jesus regularly reminded people of a realm beyond this world. During His trial before Pilate, He declared, "My kingdom is not of this world."

Why would Jesus mention this otherworldly concept to Pilate, His judge? Pilate stood as the one man who could either free Jesus or sentence Him to death. Pilate sought to determine if Jesus planned to conspire against the Roman government. Jesus had other plans in mind. He knew His outcome and His destination. Jesus could trust in a kingdom far greater than this world offers, a positive reminder for our lives today.

Share your experience now at
www.ThirstNoMoreBook.com.

"Everyone on the side of truth listens to me."
—John 18:37

As Jesus stood before Pilate, He was asked if He believed He was a king. In His response, Jesus noted, "Everyone on the side of truth listens to me."

The idea of "listening" in this context includes more than merely hearing. Listening involves comprehension plus application. Those who genuinely seek truth do not do so to satisfy human curiosity. Instead, the pursuit and discovery of truth leads to a life of holy living. Why? Because Jesus is the truth. To listen to Him is to obey Him. To obey Him is to become increasingly like Him, dedicated and progressively more holy in the process.

If you desire truth, you do well. If you find truth, you do better. If you live truth, you are truly listening to Christ.

Share your experience now at
www.ThirstNoMoreBook.com.

"What is truth?"
—John 18:38

One of the most famous lines of Scripture is Pilate's question to Jesus, "What is truth?" Provocative and multilayered in meaning, Pilate the judge stands caught between friends, enemies, and a man who claims to be the Messiah. Rather than genuinely seek the answer to his question, Pilate submitted to the pressures of the chanting audience to give Jesus over for crucifixion.

Yet Pilate's question stands before us today, "What is truth?" Truth is found in Jesus. We know this, yet overlook the power of this revelation. Take a moment to remember afresh the joy of knowing truth through Christ, in first realizing questions do have answers and life has an Answer in knowing God through His Son, Jesus the Christ.

Share your experience now at
www.ThirstNoMoreBook.com.

"Pilate took Jesus and had him flogged."
—John 19:1

Jesus endured pain on our behalf. We often think only of the Cross, with its nails and crown of thorns. But Jesus suffered much more. The Roman practice of flogging involved a short leather whip, often braided with small lead balls or chips of bone. The Jewish custom was 40 lashes minus 1. Romans held no such tradition. We do not know how long Christ's beating took place. We do know it was excruciating.

Why this suffering? For us. As each lash crossed Christ's back, His thoughts were on those of us throughout the ages who would receive forgiveness of sin through His sacrifice. Bleeding and broken, His body was broken to rescue us. He bore our shame; let us not fear suffering for His name.

Share your experience now at
www.ThirstNoMoreBook.com.

December 5

"They shouted, 'Crucify! Crucify!'"
—John 19:6

Pilate presented a bruised and bloodied Jesus before the chief priests and their officials. Jesus stood wearing a crown of thorns and purple robe. These symbols of authority covered Him in mockery. He was not only beaten; He was mocked.

This verbal abuse hurled upon Jesus hurt deeply. He had spoken words of life; now He received words of death. His opponents shouted, "Crucify!" They called not only for punishment; their goal was murder. Remember His pain in our place. As we reflect, we renew our resolve to follow Him. No matter the cost or considerations, His will must be our will, His life was exchanged to give us life. Our lives must reflect our gratitude, marked by holy living for our Holy Lord.

Share your experience now at
www.ThirstNoMoreBook.com.

"He claimed to be the Son of God."
—John 19:7

Jesus claimed to be the Son of God. His followers knew this; so did His enemies. According to their law, Jesus deserved death for blasphemy. To His opponents, the claim incited fury; to Pilate, the claim elicited fear. Jesus and Pilate faced off; one held the actual power of life and death, the other thought He held the same power. Yet our Lord made clear Pilate's power only existed because it had been given from above.

We often believe we have power to choose what to do with Jesus. The truth is we would have no ability to choose if not given by God. Let us not side with the crowd but with Christ. He not only claimed to be the Son of God, He is.

Share your experience now at
www.ThirstNoMoreBook.com.

"Carrying his own cross."
—John 19:17

Jesus had taught His followers to take up their cross and follow Him. Now He carried His own cross, literally, toward His gruesome death. Once again, He not only spoke truth; He lived it. To complete His mission required maturity; to fulfill His call required commitment.

We fall guilty of claiming the call of Christ is only a call to peace and joy, forgiveness and heaven. Though true, the call is costly. It cost Jesus His life. The call cost Him humiliation before those He had healed. The call cost Him torture before those He had taught. The call of Christ brings life, but comes at a price. He carried His own cross. He calls us to do the same.

Share your experience now at
www.ThirstNoMoreBook.com.

DECEMBER 8

"Here is your mother."
—John 19:27

Christ loved to the end. As He gasped for breath while upon the Cross, He looked down at His mother Mary in mercy. She had faithfully received the message announcing His coming. His mother had held Him the day of His birth in the manger. She had helped Him walk, mended clothing, cooked His meals. She stood by Him in life, and now she stood by Him in death.

In a closing act of kindness, Jesus looked to John. He was the only disciple at the Cross. He was the one. Looking at His mother, Jesus spoke, "Woman, here is your son." To John, "Here is your mother." The "disciple whom Jesus loved" would care for her. Let us love as He loved.

Share your experience now at
www.ThirstNoMoreBook.com.

"I am thirsty."
—John 19:28

J esus lived the Father's will up to the moment of His last earthly breath. In the agony of His final minutes in this world, He spoke words that both reflected His humanity and fulfilled the prophecies concerning the Messiah: "I am thirsty."

In His humanity, Jesus had endured hours of suffering without the smallest cup of water. His body ached for vital fluids. Yet in satisfaction of God's prediction, He asked for a drink. Once His mission stood completed, He could then and only then announce, "It is finished." His example expresses His will for us—our lives exist to fulfill the Father's will. Only when completed will we depart and be with Him, which is better by far. Are you living your purpose today?

Share your experience now at
www.ThirstNoMoreBook.com.

"It is finished."
—John 19:30

Three simple words conclude the final seconds of Jesus' mission on earth. We, likewise, are given but a fleeting few days to live out our Father's will. We may lack the ability to know our final breath as Jesus did, but we can acknowledge eternity is near, whether today or years into the future.

When we come to our final breath, will we look back with regret or forward with anticipation? For many of us, the answer includes aspects of both. Jesus lived a no-regret life, an all-consuming mission to please His Father and accomplish His will. We stand challenged to imitate Christ. We must live well in order to die well. We must pursue His glory, unrelenting until our "It is finished."

Share your experience now at
www.ThirstNoMoreBook.com.

"The body of Jesus."
—John 19:38

Jesus had died, yet His body remained. Joseph of Arimathea asked permission to bury His body. Why? He was a disciple, though secretly for fear of the Jewish leaders. Further, he had access to a nearby tomb. He likely felt much respect for Jesus and sought to show respect through a proper burial.

We are never told the beginning of Joseph's story nor its ending. Yet in a few words, much is communicated. This man had believed quietly, but now he came boldly before his ruler Pilate to bury His true Ruler. Washing away blood and dirt, He would understand perhaps more than anyone the power of Christ's body upon His resurrection. He died, He was buried, yet He lives again.

Share your experience now at
www.ThirstNoMoreBook.com.

"He was accompanied by Nicodemus."
—John 19:39

Nicodemus had come to Jesus earlier with the question, "How can a man be born again?" Jesus spoke to Him about everlasting life. Now Nicodemus held the body of Jesus in his hands. He wrapped strips of cloth, poured on spices, and laid His corpse in the tomb. The one who had raised the dead was now dead Himself.

As soldiers rolled the stone over the entrance, Nicodemus said what he thought was a final good-bye to the One who had greeted him that night long ago. Little did he know what would happen to begin the next week. The words Jesus spoke would come true in a way beyond all comprehension. Thank God for Nicodemus. In his first encounter with the Lord we hear about being "born again."

Share your experience now at
www.ThirstNoMoreBook.com.

"Peter...went straight into the tomb."
—John 20:6

Peter was not the first to discover the empty tomb, but he was the first to enter it. Upon his arrival, he headed directly to where his Master's body had laid. There were strips of linen. The cloth that had covered Christ's head rested neatly folded. His body was gone, but not in the manner of a corpse that had been stolen.

There were multiple witnesses of the empty tomb. There was no doubt a body had been placed behind the stone; there was also no doubt the body was no longer there that early Sunday morning. The disciple who had denied knowing Christ stood exactly where his Lord's corpse had rested. His followers were about to realize this mysterious disappearance was proof of their Master's resurrection.

Share your experience now at
www.ThirstNoMoreBook.com.

"Why are you crying?"
—John 20:15

As Mary wept at Jesus' tomb, she began a conversation with a man she believed at first was the gardener. This gardener, unknown to her, was the risen Jesus. He began by asking, "Woman, why are you crying?" The reader, knowing this man is Jesus, also knows He already knows the answer to His question. So why does He ask?

We are not told the complete answer, but we can observe Jesus uses this question to begin a conversation, one that ends with Mary recognizing Jesus. In our lives, Jesus knows the answer to every question of our hearts. Why does He ask? To join us in conversation—conversation that will lead us to a greater recognition of the risen Jesus.

Share your experience now at
www.ThirstNoMoreBook.com.

"Jesus said to her, 'Mary.'"
—John 20:16

Jesus knows our name. We realize this, but we likely fail to realize one incredible application of this providential knowledge—He speaks our name. When Mary spoke with Jesus in the garden, she first thought He was a garden keeper. It was not until He spoke her name—"Mary"—that she realized it was her Lord Jesus.

When Jesus speaks to us, He speaks our name. He speaks in our heart-language, to our needs, at our level. No other person or power can compare to the unmatched connection He makes when we pray and He "speaks our name." If you feel far from the Savior today, call out to Him. And listen for His love. Listen in your heart and mind, for He is waiting to address you by your name.

Share your experience now at
www.ThirstNoMoreBook.com.

"She...cried out in Aramaic, 'Rabboni!'"
—John 20:16

When Mary recognized the risen Jesus, emotion swept through every fiber of her body. Instantly, she responded, "Rabboni!" This votive response provides a miniscule glimpse into relationship between Jesus and one of His earliest followers. First, Mary answers in Aramaic. "Rabboni" expressed Mary's heart-language, the tongue of her first thoughts as well as a language Jesus knew. That Jesus hears and understands us in our heart-languages provides powerful comfort to us today.

Further, "Rabboni" correctly identifies Jesus as teacher. Jesus is not a gardener, nor is He still in the garden tomb. He is the Teacher, He is alive, and He continues to speak to us today. His life and message transforms us. Let His truth teach us anew this day.

Share your experience now at
www.ThirstNoMoreBook.com.

"I have seen the Lord!"
—John 20:18

After experiencing the risen Lord, Mary's message was, "I have *seen* the Lord! [emphasis added]" Her brief witness bears a myriad of insights that reflect Christ's greatness. First, it reflects her personal connection with Christ. He is not a King far away but a friend to those He loves. Second, *seen* unveils the direct nature of the risen Christ. Mary did not dream of Jesus alive nor did she experience a vision. She *saw* Him.

Finally, Mary calls Jesus the Lord. The language makes clear her belief in Jesus as God's Messiah. Only the Messiah could save His people from their sins. Will we declare through our lives and lips, "I have seen the Lord"? Let us follow Mary's example in sharing the living Jesus.

Share your experience now at
www.ThirstNoMoreBook.com.

"Peace be with you."
—John 20:19

When Jesus first appeared to His disciples, He greeted them with, "Peace be with you." The intention behind this phrase is seemingly obscure. But the prophet Zechariah revealed Israel's coming king would "proclaim peace to the nations." By greeting His followers with peace, Jesus connected His resurrection with the prophecies of a future Messiah who would bring peace to earth.

The opposite of peace is unrest–war, conflict, insecurity, or fear. Christ offers peace. Peace with us. Take a moment to embrace the peace, the rest, He offers our souls. Anticipate the coming peace of His future kingdom, His eternal peace. Hear Him say, to you His follower at this moment, "Peace be with you."

Share your experience now at
www.ThirstNoMoreBook.com.

"I am sending you."
—John 20:21

The risen Jesus stood before His followers for the first time since His resurrection. His first instructions? "I am sending you."

He suffered so we could be sent. His Spirit empowers us to carry His message of love to the most diverse of peoples, from inside our offices at work to the ends of the earth. In generations past and present, some have misunderstood the purpose of holiness to mean separation from the world. Whether monastics or modernists secluded from society, well-intending people have separated rather than being sent for the Savior.

Our proper response to the living Christ is service to others rather than separation from them. Do not move away from those who need His love today. Step out in faith. Be sent. "I am sending you."

Share your experience now at
www.ThirstNoMoreBook.com.

"Receive the Holy Spirit."
—John 20:22

The disciples of Jesus were the first recipients of the Holy Spirit after the resurrection of Christ. In His initial appearance to His followers, He shared a gift: "Receive the Holy Spirit."

While this situation was unique to this encounter, one aspect is similar—the Holy Spirit is a gift. Many have been trained to think the Spirit of God is a Holy "Ghost," an unseen power, but rarely speak of Him as Jesus did, a gift.

Right now, pause on the gift of God's Spirit in you. The Holy Spirit, part of the Triune God, lives within you. There is nothing greater God could give but Himself. Live in His power today. As the disciples of old, savor the risen Christ. Live in the power of His Spirit.

Share your experience now at
www.ThirstNoMoreBook.com.

"Stop doubting and believe."
—John 20:27

Thomas did not sit in the room when the living Jesus first appeared to the disciples. Upon his return, Thomas rejected the nonsense of Jesus being alive. He refused to believe unless Jesus directly appeared to Him.

A few days later, Jesus did. Thomas received a series of direct commands that ended with "Stop doubting and believe." We often know what Jesus expects of us. His Word and His Spirit have shown us the way. Yet we doubt. We require more evidence, just as Thomas did.

Friend, Jesus has given His command for our doubts: "Stop doubting." He has also provided the answer to our doubts: "Believe." Sometimes, we do not need more proof. We need more faith. The answer to doubt is not always evidence. The answer to doubt is belief.

Share your experience now at
www.ThirstNoMoreBook.com.

"My Lord and My God!"
—John 20:28

When Thomas witnessed the risen Jesus, he had but one response: "My Lord and My God!" Both terms, "Lord" and "God", reflect important aspects of Christ's character. As "Lord," He is the sovereign ruler of the universe. As "God," He is recognized as Creator or all things, Sustainer of life, all-powerful One.

The response of Thomas was brief, yet accurate. Jesus is worthy of our highest adoration; He is the Creator of all things. The more we see Jesus as redeemer of life and maker of life, the greater our awe as we worship the only true God. Our view of life derives from our view of God. Our view of God derives from our view of Christ.

Share your experience now at
www.ThirstNoMoreBook.com.

December 23

*"Blessed are those who have not seen
and yet have believed."*
—John 20:29

We are blessed. We have not seen and yet have believed. This blessing applied to those who had believed the news of the risen Christ at that time and extends to us today. When we believe, we are blessed.

Why are we considered blessed? One reason is faith. To believe in the unseen requires faith. Faith sustains us in times of weakness, strengthens our resolve in the face of conflict, and shields us from the limitations of the visible world. Apart from Christ, faith is impossible; apart from faith, Christ-like living is impossible. When faith moves us to action, lives are changed and eternity impacts us. Where faith exists, hope exists; where hope exists, love lives. Faith, hope, and love remain, providing a blessing today.

Share your experience now at
www.ThirstNoMoreBook.com.

"These are written that you may believe."
—John 20:31

John notes toward the end of his Gospel that Jesus performed many more miracles than those he had recorded. So why did John select the signs he shared? "These are written that you may believe."

We often view miracles as evidence of the supernatural or of God's invisible hand at work. John had a somewhat different purpose, as did Jesus. The miracles of Christ were recorded by pen on parchment to point us toward the eternal reality of Jesus as Messiah. Water turned to wine means little apart from revealing the identity of Jesus. Even reviving Lazarus from the dead holds limited impact apart from the person who accomplished the marvel. Sometimes we don't need a miracle; we just need to look to the Messiah.

Share your experience now at
www.ThirstNoMoreBook.com.

"By believing you may have life in his name."
—John 20:31

As the Apostle John wraps up his Gospel, he hones in on the purpose of his effort. It begins with belief. John clearly wrote to persuade. His goal was to direct attention to Jesus as the Christ. But belief was never intended as the final goal. The goal was and is life.

Life is more than breathing or a pulse. Life from John's perspective is vibrant relationship with the maker of life, Jesus Christ. This, too, explains why John writes that we can have life "in his name." We can exist apart from belief in the risen Christ; but we cannot experience life apart from His name. Belief is the first step to true life, life abundant and life eternal.

Share your experience now at
www.ThirstNoMoreBook.com.

December 26

"The disciples did not realize it was Jesus."
—John 21:4

How could the disciples not realize they were looking right at Jesus? The distance to shore from their boat could explain the scenario. Then Jesus spoke to the seven disciples and they still did not identify Him. It was only once they had caught an unexpected number of fish that John recognized, "It is the Lord."

Sometimes the sight of Jesus or even His voice is not enough to capture our attention. Only once we experience the unexpected do we direct attention to Him. Jesus used this time to confront Peter's earlier failures and restore him in his calling. Our Lord is standing near to speak to us today, too. Look for Him. Listen for Him. Watch for Christ in the unexpected.

Share your experience now at
www.ThirstNoMoreBook.com.

"It is the Lord!"
—John 21:7

When Peter's eyes were opened to Jesus, life changed. He was no longer a fisherman; he was a follower. He was no longer a sailor; he was a swimmer. People often speak of developing our spiritual lives. But Peter exemplifies one who left everything to pursue Christ. He had no desire to grow a little; he intended to give all.

One of our deepest temptations is to give Christ part of our allegiance, but not all. This is not His desire. If we serve with only halfhearted devotion, Jesus will not be honored, but dishonored. Once He reveals Himself to us, the Lord expects devotion from us. Let us follow Him passionately today. Let us dive in as Peter: "It is the Lord!"

Share your experience now at
www.ThirstNoMoreBook.com.

"Do you love me more than these?"
—John 21:15

If Jesus were to ask each of us if we love Him, our instant reaction would likely be, "Yes, of course I do!" This, too, was the response of Peter. Except Jesus asked Peter this question three times. By the third time, Peter was hurt. He felt his loyalty, not just his love, was being questioned.

But sometimes Jesus must repeat a question to us on multiple occasions to capture our attention. Once is not enough, nor is a second time. If God seems to be asking you the same question repeatedly, stop. There is an important message He needs you to hear. Only when you receive this message and obey it will you be prepared to serve on the path Christ has prepared for you.

Share your experience now at
www.ThirstNoMoreBook.com.

"Follow me!"
—John 21:22

"Follow me!" Jesus often used these words initially to call His disciples. Yet on one occasion, He used this phrase to a person who had already served among His closest followers, Simon Peter.

Peter had recently denied Jesus three separate times in one night. He had been a follower. He had become a deserter. After His resurrection, Jesus again extended His call to this resilient fisherman, who soon became the premier leader in the earliest Christian church. Peter later would follow Christ to martyrdom, revealing his full allegiance to his Lord. Even if we have denied Jesus, He still calls us to follow Him. He is the God of second and third chances. We likewise must be servants who accept His second and third calls.

Share your experience now at
www.ThirstNoMoreBook.com.

"Lord, what about him?"
—John 21:21

Comparison is a universal human characteristic. We seek to prove ourselves either better than or worse than those around us in every conceivable manner possible. Peter was no exception. When called to "feed my sheep," Peter turned back to the apostle John and asked, "Lord, what about him?"

Christ's response speaks volumes to us in this moment. Rather than participating in comparisons, Jesus quickly dismissed Peter's question and reaffirmed, "You must follow me." Our eyes must not stray to the next servant of God and his or her accomplishments. God has His own plans for them. Instead, our eyes are to be fixed on Jesus our Master. We exist to please Him, not compete with others. We must follow Christ and Christ alone.

Share your experience now at
www.ThirstNoMoreBook.com.

"Even the whole world would not have room."
—John 21:25

John ended his words with the statement, "Jesus did many other things as well. If every one of them were written down, I suppose that even the whole world would not have room for the books that would be written." We are given but a glimpse of Christ's power. He offers much more than He yet has revealed.

Do we walk in awareness of the limitless power of our Lord? He seeks to perform much more in our lives. Let us ask Him to transform our lives and those around us. Let us seek to spread His fame to the end of the earth; His glory from sunrise to sunset. Let us end our words together knowing His works exceed more than we can imagine.

Share your experience now at
www.ThirstNoMoreBook.com.

Thirst No More

Book + Community = Clean Water and Changed Lives

Every time you purchase a copy of *Thirst No More*, a portion of your purchase helps to fund a new freshwater well, in Haiti, or elsewhere in a thirsty world, through Living Water International (www .water.cc).

Living Water International

Living Water International (LWI) exists to demonstrate the love of God by helping communities acquire desperately needed clean water, and to experience "living water"—the gospel of Jesus Christ—which alone satisfies the deepest thirst.

Nearly 20 years ago, we set out to help the church in North America be the hands and feet of Jesus by serving the poorest of the poor. More than 1 billion people in the world live on less than a dollar a day. There are 884 million people who lack access to safe drinking water.

For all practical purposes, these statistics refer to the same people; around the world, communities are trapped in debilitating poverty because they constantly suffer from water-related diseases and parasites, and/or because they spend long stretches of their time carrying water over long distances.

In response to this need, we implement participatory, community-based water solutions in developing countries. Since we started, we've completed more than 9,000 water projects (and counting!) for communities in 26 countries.

It all began in 1990, when a group from Houston, Texas, traveled to Kenya and saw the desperate need for clean drinking water. They returned to Houston and founded a 501(c)3 nonprofit. The fledgling organization equipped and trained a team of Kenyan drillers, and LWI Kenya began operations the next year under the direction of a national board. That pattern continues today; we train, consult, and equip local people to implement solutions in their own countries.

Remembering the life-changing nature of that first trip in 1990, we also lead hundreds of volunteers on missions trips each year, working with local communities, under the leadership of nationals, to implement water projects. It's hard to know which lives are changed more—those "serving" or those "being served." Our training programs in shallow well drilling, pump repair, and hygiene education have equipped thousands of volunteers and professionals in the basics of integrated water solutions since 1997.

HERE'S HOW IT WORKS.

A portion of the proceeds from this project will benefit the clean water initiatives of Living Water International. Learn more at www.water.cc.

1. You purchase a copy of *Thirst No More*.
2. Read today's entry.
3. Communicate your response at www .ThirstNoMoreBook.com (on your computer, phone, or other device).
4. Share your response with your friends and ask them to purchase a copy of *Thirst No More*.

Soon, we'll be reading reflections of how God is working in our lives with a community of friends all around the world.

At the same time, we'll also be helping contribute to the well we are working together to fund in Haiti, sharing stories of progress along the way.

The costs break down as follows:

- One book's contribution provides clean water to one person for two months.

- Involve six other friends by giving copies of *Thirst No More* and provide clean water to one person for one year.

- Donate more as you are able through our online community's secure donation page.

If we all give a little, we can change a lot.
Our goal is one well to provide clean water to 5,000 people in Haiti (by December 31, 2012).

Wouldn't it be great to say we helped an entire village *Thirst No More?*

New Hope® Publishers is a division of WMU®, an international organization that challenges Christian believers to understand and be radically involved in God's mission. For more information about WMU, go to www.wmu.com. More information about New Hope books may be found at www.newhopedigital.com. New Hope books may be purchased at your local bookstore.

Use the QR reader on your smartphone to visit us online at www.newhopedigital.com

If you've been blessed by this book, we would like to hear your story. The publisher and author welcome your comments and suggestions at: newhopereader@wmu.org.

Related Titles from New Hope:

**Called and Accountable
52-Week Devotional**
*Henry T. Blackaby and
Norman C. Blackaby
with Dana Blackaby*
ISBN-13: 978-1-59669-214-5 • $14.99

Not in My Town
*Dillon Burroughs and
Charles Powell*
ISBN-13: 978-1-59669-301-2 • $19.99

NEW HOPE
PUBLISHERS
Available in bookstores everywhere

For information about these books or any New Hope product,
visit www.newhopedigital.com.